# abc BRITISH RAILWAYS ATLAS

## M. G. Ball

D0519741

IAN ALLAN Publishing

First published 1995

ISBN 0 7110 2339 5

Published by Ian Allan Publishing

an imprint of Ian Allan Ltd, Terminal House, Station Approach, Shepperton, Surrey TW17 8AS.

Printed by Ian Allan Printing Ltd, Coombelands House, Coombelands Lane, Addlestone, Weybridge, Surrey KT15 1HY.

*Cover photographs courtesy Brian Morrison*

## KEY TO ATLAS

⎯⎯◯⎯⎯ Railway line & station

⎯⎯✕⎯⎯ Proposed station

⎯⎯⊕⎯⎯ Unadvertised or excursion station

⎯⎯●⎯⎯ Other location

============= Proposed line

P.F.C. Proposed for closure

O.O.U. Out of use

Ⓣ Tourist line. Seasonal service

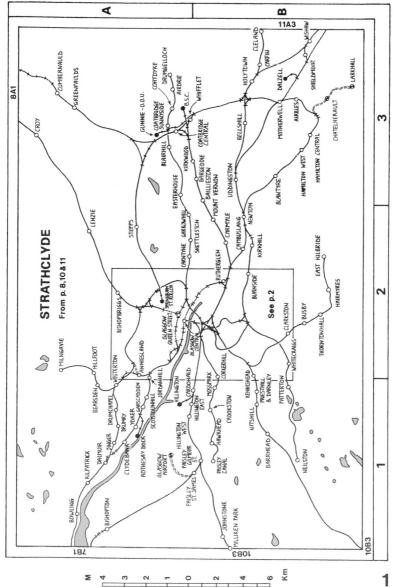

# STRATHCLYDE

From p. 8,10 &11

A

B

3

2

1

See p.2

CUMBERNAULD
GREENFAULDS
CROY
LENZIE
CORTDYKE
DRUMGELLOCH
AIRDRIE
GUNNIE -O.O.U.
COATBRIDGE
SUNNYSIDE
WHIFFLET
B.S.C.
COATBRIDGE
CENTRAL
BLAIRHILL
KIRKWOOD
BARGEDDIE
BAILLIESTON
EASTERHOUSE
GARROWHILL
MOUNT VERNON
UDDINGSTON
CARNTYNE
SHETTLESTON
CARMYLE
NEWTON
STEPS
CAMBUSLANG
KIRKHILL
SPRINGBURN
BARNHILL
RUTHERGLEN
BISHOPBRIGGS
GLASGOW QUEEN STREET
GLASGOW CENTRAL
BURNSIDE
EAST KILBRIDE
HAIRMYRES
CLARKSTON
BUSBY
THORNTONHALL
WESTERTON
ANNIESLAND
JORDANHILL
HYNDLAND
SCOTSTOUNHILL
GARSCADDEN
YOKER
DRUMRY
DRUMCHAPEL
BEARSDEN
HILLFOOT
MILNGAVIE
HILLINGTON
EAST
HILLINGTON
WEST
CARDONALD
MOSSPARK
CORKERHILL
KENNISHEAD
NITSHILL
PRIESTHILL
& DARNLEY
PATTERTON
CROOKSTON
HAWKHEAD
BARRHEAD
NEILSTON
SINGER
CLYDEBANK
DALMUIR
KILPATRICK
BOWLING
BISHOPTON
ROTHESAY DOCK
GLASGOW AIRPORT
PAISLEY
GILMOUR ST.
PAISLEY
ST. JAMES
PAISLEY CANAL
JOHNSTONE
MILLIKEN PARK
CLELAND
WISHAW
CARFIN
HOLYTOWN
MOTHERWELL
AIRBLES
DALZELL
SHIELDMUIR
LARKHALL
CHATELHERAULT
BELLSHILL
HAMILTON WEST
HAMILTON CENTRAL
BLANTYRE

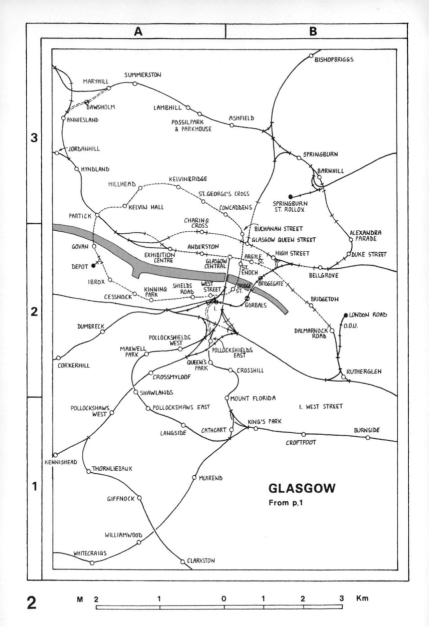

A | B

3

2

1

BISHOPBRIGGS
SUMMERSTON
MARYHILL
DAWSHOLM
LAMBHILL
ASHFIELD
ANNIESLAND
POSSILPARK
& PARKHOUSE
SPRINGBURN
JORDANHILL
BARNHILL
HYNDLAND
HILLHEAD
KELVINBRIDGE
ST.GEORGE'S CROSS
SPRINGBURN
ST. ROLLOX
KELVIN HALL
COWCADDENS
PARTICK
CHARING
CROSS
BUCHANAN STREET
ALEXANDRA
PARADE
GLASGOW QUEEN STREET
DUKE STREET
ANDERSTON
HIGH STREET
GOVAN
EXHIBITION
CENTRE
ARGYLE
ST.
DEPOT
GLASGOW
CENTRAL
ST.
ENOCH
BELLGROVE
IBROX
SHIELDS
ROAD
WEST
STREET
BRIDGE
ST.
BRIDGEGATE
KINNING
PARK
CESSNOCK
I.
GORBALS
BRIDGETON
LONDON ROAD
DUMBRECK
O.O.U.
DALMARNOCK
ROAD
POLLOCKSHIELDS
WEST
MAXWELL
PARK
POLLOCKSHIELDS
EAST
CORKERHILL
QUEEN'S
PARK
CROSSHILL
RUTHERGLEN
CROSSMYLOOF
SHAWLANDS
MOUNT FLORIDA
I. WEST STREET
POLLOCKSHAWS
WEST
POLLOCKSHAWS EAST
KING'S PARK
LANGSIDE
CATHCART
BURNSIDE
CROFTOOT
KENNISHEAD
THORNLIEBANK
MUIREND
GLASGOW
From p.1
GIFFNOCK
WILLIAMWOOD
WHITECRAIGS
CLARKSTON

M 2 | 1 | 0 | 1 | 2 | 3 Km

2

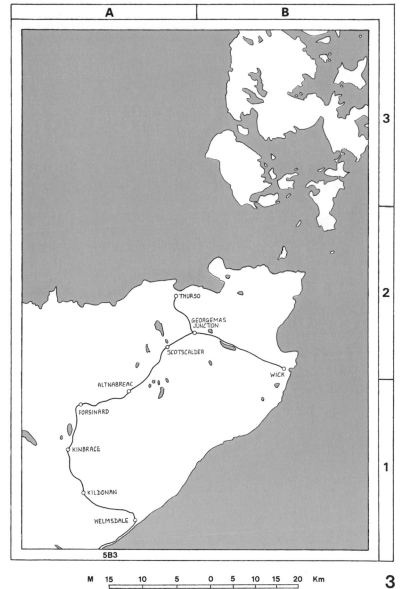

A          B

3

2

THURSO
GEORGEMAS
JUNCTION
SCOTSCALDER
ALTNABREAC                    WICK
FORSINARD
KINBRACE
KILDONAN
HELMSDALE

5B3

M   15   10   5   0   5   10   15   20   Km

3

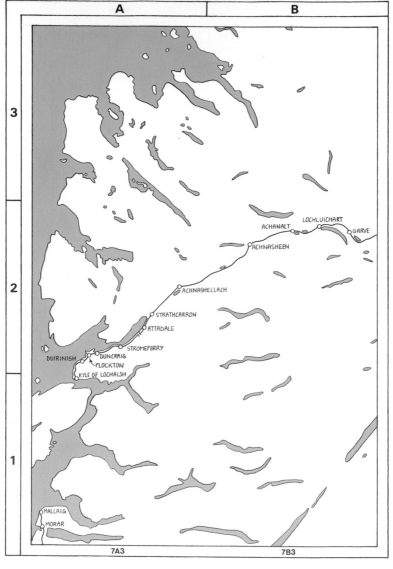

3

2

1

GARVE
LOCHLUICHART
ACHANALT
ACHNASHEEN
ACHNASHELLACH
STRATHCARRON
ATTADALE
STROMEFERRY
DUNCRAIG
DUIRINISH
PLOCKTON
KYLE OF LOCHALSH

MALLAIG
MORAR

4

M  15    10    5    0    5    10    20   Km

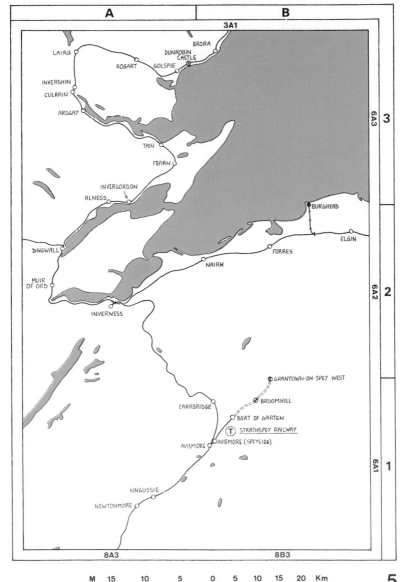

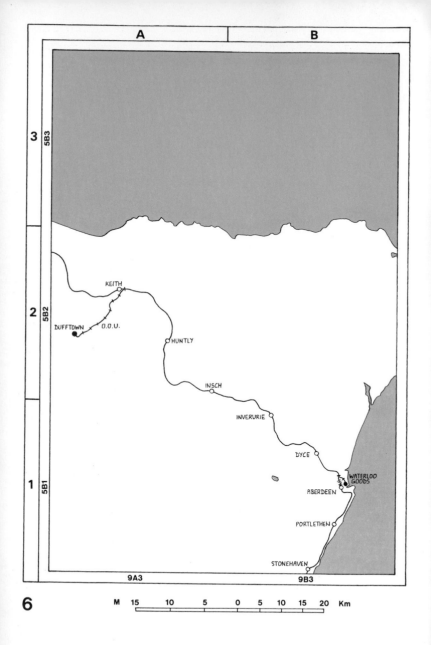

KEITH

DUFFTOWN • D.O.U.

HUNTLY

INSCH

INVERURIE

DYCE

WATERLOO GOODS

ABERDEEN

PORTLETHEN

STONEHAVEN

A          B

3  5B3

2  5B2

1  5B1

9A3          9B3

6

M  15  10  5  0  5  10  15  20  Km

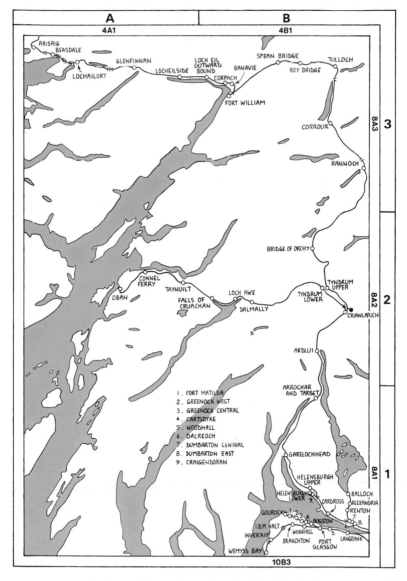

ARISAIG
BEASDALE
LOCHAILORT
GLENFINNAN
LOCHEILSIDE
LOCH EIL OUTWARD BOUND
CORPACH
BANAVIE
SPEAN BRIDGE
ROY BRIDGE
TULLOCH
FORT WILLIAM
CORROUR
RANNOCH
BRIDGE OF ORCHY
CONNEL FERRY
TAYNUILT
OBAN
FALLS OF CRUACHAN
LOCH AWE
DALMALLY
TYNDRUM UPPER
TYNDRUM LOWER
CRIANLARICH
ARDLUI
ARROCHAR AND TARBET
GARELOCHHEAD
HELENSBURGH UPPER
HELENSBURGH LOWER
CARDROSS
BALLOCH
ALEXANDRIA
RENTON
GOUROCK
BOGSTON
I.B.M. HALT
INVERKIP
WHINHILL
BRANCHTON
PORT GLASGOW
LANGBANK
WEMYSS BAY

1. FORT MATILDA
2. GREENOCK WEST
3. GREENOCK CENTRAL
4. CARTSDYKE
5. WOODHALL
6. DALREOCH
7. DUMBARTON CENTRAL
8. DUMBARTON EAST
9. CRAIGENDORAN

M  15  10  5  0  5  10  15  20  Km

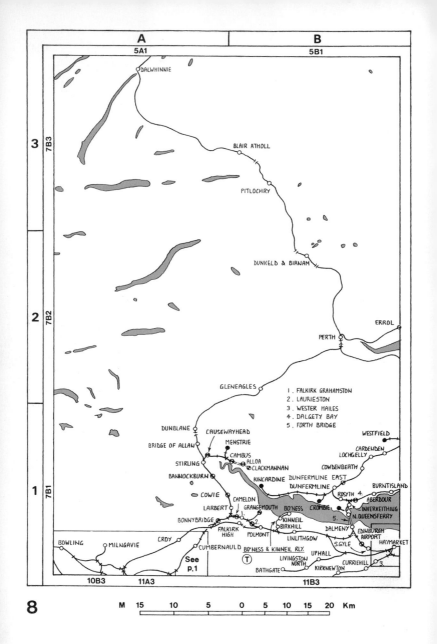

3    7B3

2    7B2

1    7B1

DALWHINNIE

BLAIR ATHOLL

PITLOCHRY

DUNKELD & BIRNAM

ERROL

PERTH

GLENEAGLES

1. FALKIRK GRAHAMSTON
2. LAURIESTON
3. WESTER HAILES
4. DALGETY BAY
5. FORTH BRIDGE

DUNBLANE
BRIDGE OF ALLAN
CAUSEWAYHEAD
MENSTRIE
CAMBUS
STIRLING
ALLOA
CLACKMANNAN
BANNOCKBURN
KINCARDINE

WESTFIELD
CARDENDEN
LOCHGELLY
COWDENBEATH
DUNFERMLINE EAST
DUNFERMLINE
ROSYTH    4
CROMBIE
BURNTISLAND
ABERDOUR
INVERKEITHING
N.QUEENSFERRY

COWIE
LARBERT
CAMELON
GRANGEMOUTH
BO'NESS
BONNYBRIDGE
FALKIRK
HIGH
KINNEIL
BIRKHILL
DALMENY
DALMENY
EDINBURGH
AIRPORT

BOWLING
MILNGAVIE
CRDY
CUMBERNAULD
POLMONT
LINLITHGOW
S.GYLE
HAYMARKET

See
p.1
BO'NESS & KINNEIL RLY.
(T)

LIVINGSTON
NORTH
UPHALL
CURRIEHILL
3

BATHGATE
KIRKNEWTON

8

M  15  10  5  0  5  10  15  20  Km

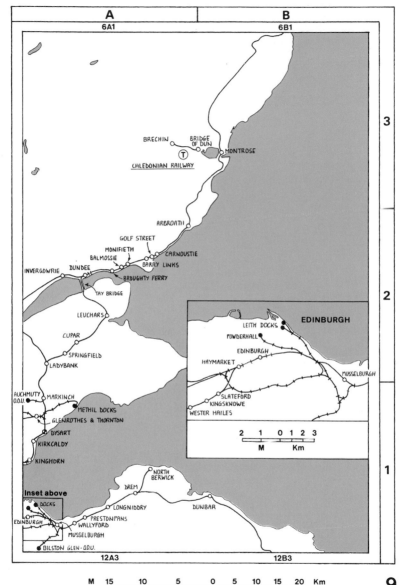

BRECHIN — BRIDGE OF DUN

(T) MONTROSE

CHLEDONIAN RAILWAY

ARBROATH

GOLF STREET

MONIFIETH

BALMOSSIE CARNOUSTIE

INVERGOWRIE DUNDEE BARRY LINKS

BROUGHTY FERRY

TAY BRIDGE

LEUCHARS

CUPAR

SPRINGFIELD

LADYBANK

AUCHMUTY O.D.U. MARKINCH

METHIL DOCKS

GLENROTHES & THORNTON

DYSART

KIRKCALDY

KINGHORN

LEITH DOCKS EDINBURGH

POWDERHALL

EDINBURGH

HAYMARKET

MUSSELBURGH

SLATEFORD

KINGSKNOWE

WESTER HAILES

2 1 0 1 2 3

M Km

NORTH BERWICK

DREM

Inset above

DOCKS LONGNIDDRY DUNBAR

EDINBURGH PRESTONPANS

WALLYFORD

MUSSELBURGH

BILSTON GLEN - O.D.U.

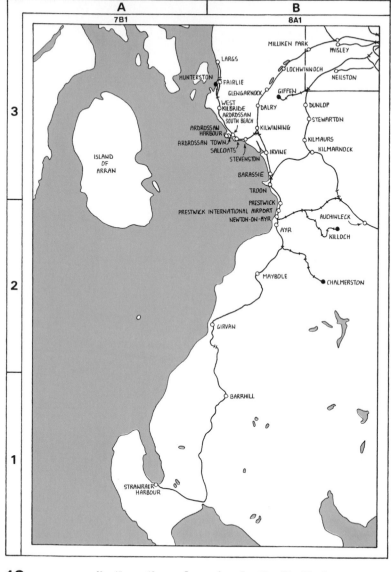

MILLIKEN PARK
PAISLEY

LARGS
LOCHWINNOCH
NEILSTON

HUNTERSTON
FAIRLIE
GLENGARNOCK GIFFEN
WEST DALRY DUNLOP
KILBRIDE
ARDROSSAN STEWARTON
SOUTH BEACH
KILWINNING
ARDROSSAN
HARBOUR KILMAURS
ARDROSSAN TOWN KILMARNOCK
SALCOATS IRVINE
STEVENSTON

ISLAND
OF
ARRAN

BARASSIE

TROON

PRESTWICK
PRESTWICK INTERNATIONAL AIRPORT AUCHINLECK
NEWTON-ON-AYR
AYR
KILLOCH

MAYBOLE CHALMERSTON

GIRVAN

BARRHILL

STRANRAER
HARBOUR

10

M 15 10 5 0 5 10 15 20 Km

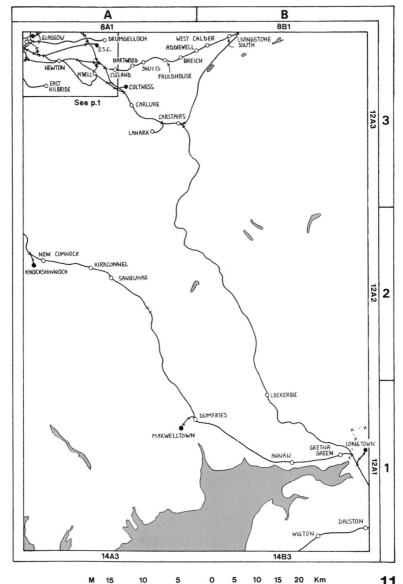

GLASGOW
DRUMGELLOCH
WEST CALDER
ADDIEWELL
LIVINGSTONE
SOUTH
B.S.C.
HARTWOOD
NEWTON
M'WELL
CLELAND
SHOTTS
BREICH
FAULDHOUSE
EAST
KILBRIDE
COLTNESS
See p.1
CARLUKE
CARSTAIRS
LANARK

NEW CUMNOCK
KIRKCONNEL
KNOCKSHINNOCH
SANQUHAR

LOCKERBIE
DUMFRIES
MAXWELLTOWN
LONGTOWN
ANNAN
GRETNA
GREEN
DALSTON
WIGTON

3
2
1

M 15 10 5 0 5 10 15 20 Km

**11**

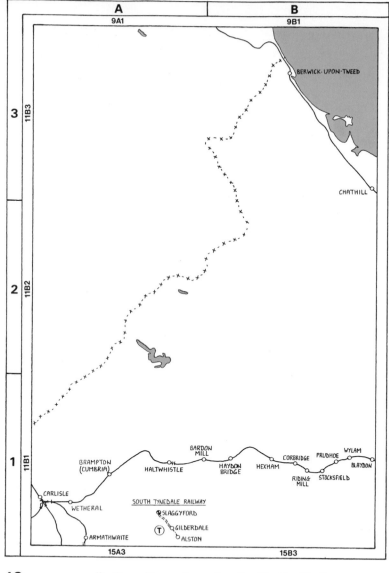

A 9A1 B 9B1

3 11B3

BERWICK-UPON-TWEED

CHATHILL

2 11B2

1 11B1

BARDON
MILL
WYLAM
BRAMPTON
(CUMBRIA) HALTWHISTLE HAYDON CORBRIDGE PRUDHOE BLAYDON
BRIDGE HEXHAM
RIDING STOCKSFIELD
CARLISLE MILL
WETHERAL
SOUTH TYNEDALE RAILWAY
SLAGGYFORD
T GILDERDALE
ARMATHWAITE ALSTON

15A3 15B3

12        M  15    10    5    0    5    10    15    20  Km

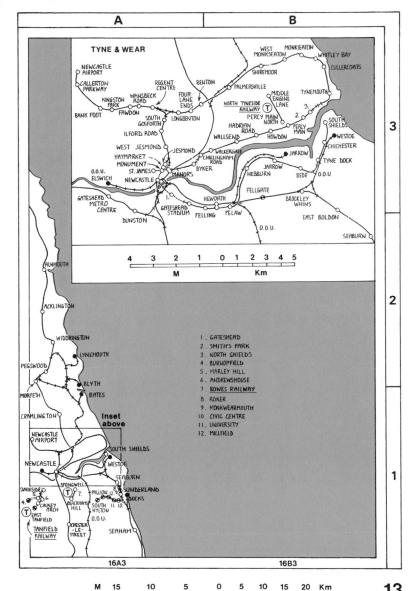

TYNE & WEAR

1. GATESHEAD
2. SMITH'S PARK
3. NORTH SHIELDS
4. BURNOPFIELD
5. MARLEY HILL
6. ANDREWSHOUSE
7. BOWES RAILWAY
8. ROKER
9. MONKWEARMOUTH
10. CIVIC CENTRE
11. UNIVERSITY
12. MILLFIELD

A          B

3

2

1

16A3                    16B3

M  15    10    5    0    5    10    15    20  Km

13

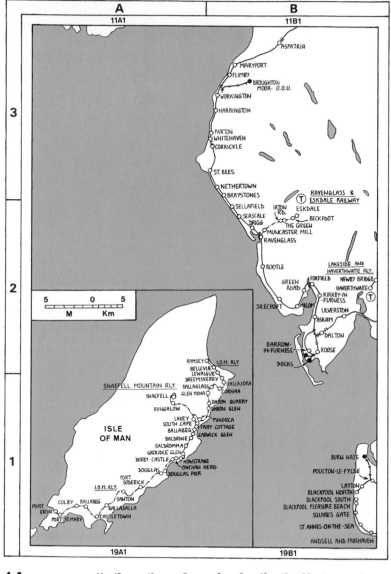

3

ASPATRIA
MARYPORT
FLIMBY
BROUGHTON MOOR- O.O.U.
WORKINGTON
HARRINGTON
PARTON
WHITEHAVEN
CORKICKLE

ST. BEES
NETHERTOWN
BRAYSTONES
SELLAFIELD
SEASCALE
DRIGG
IRTON RD.  ESKDALE
  BECKFOOT
RAVENGLASS & ESKDALE RAILWAY
THE GREEN
MUNCASTER MILL
RAVENGLASS

BOOTLE
LAKESIDE AND HAVERTHWAITE RLY.
GREEN ROAD
FOXFIELD  NEWBY BRIDGE
  HAVERTHWAITE
KIRKBY-IN-FURNESS
SILECROFT  MILLOM
  ULVERSTON
ASKAM
  DALTON
BARROW-IN-FURNESS  ROOSE
DOCKS

2

5  0  5
M  Km

RAMSEY  I.O.M. RLY.
BELLEVUE
LEWAIGUE
DREEMSKERRY
BALLAGLASS  BALLAJORA
GLEN MONA  CORNAA
SNAEFELL MOUNTAIN RLY.
SNAEFELL  DHOON QUARRY
BUNGALOW  DHOON GLEN
LAXEY  MINORCA
SOUTH CAPE  FAIRY COTTAGE
BALLABEG
BALDRINE  GARWICK GLEN
BALDROMMA
GROUDLE GLEN
DERBY CASTLE  HOWSTRAKE
DOUGLAS  ONCHAN HEAD
PORT  DOUGLAS PIER
SODERICK

ISLE OF MAN

I.O.M. RLY.
PORT  COLBY  BALLABEG
ERIN  SANTON
PORT ST.MARY  BALLASALLA
  CASTLETOWN

BURN NAZE
POULTON-LE-FYLDE
LAYTON
BLACKPOOL NORTH
BLACKPOOL SOUTH
BLACKPOOL PLEASURE BEACH
SQUIRES GATE
ST. ANNES-ON-THE-SEA
ANDSELL AND FAIRHAVEN

1

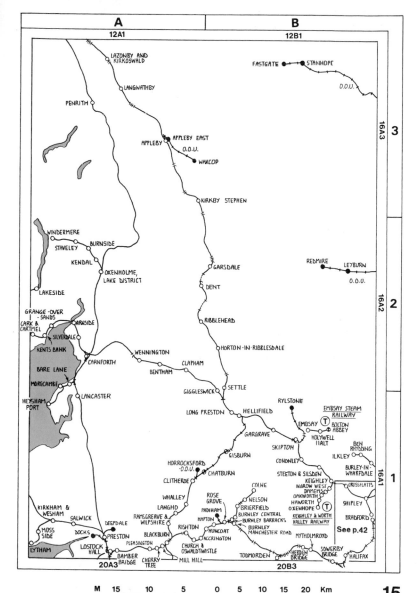

LAZONBY AND
KIRKOSWALD

LANGWATHBY

PENRITH

FASTGATE ●—●—● STANHOPE

D.O.U.

APPLEBY EAST

APPLEBY

O.O.U.

WARCOP

KIRKBY STEPHEN

WINDERMERE

BURNSIDE

STAVELEY

KENDAL

OXENHOLME,
LAKE DISTRICT

LAKESIDE

GARSDALE

DENT

RIBBLEHEAD

REDMIRE ●—●—● LEYBURN

O.O.U.

GRANGE-OVER
-SANDS

CARK &
CARTMEL

ARNSIDE

SILVERDALE

KENTS BANK

BARE LANE

MORECAMBE

HEYSHAM
PORT

CARNFORTH

WENNINGTON

BENTHAM

CLAPHAM

HORTON-IN-RIBBLESDALE

SETTLE

LANCASTER

GIGGLESWICK

RYLSTONE

LONG PRESTON

HELLIFIELD

EMBSAY STEAM
RAILWAY

GARGRAVE

EMBSAY (T)

BOLTON
ABBEY

HOLYWELL
HALT

SKIPTON

BEN
RHYDDING

HORROCKSFORD
O.O.U.

GISBURN

CHATBURN

CONONLEY

ILKLEY

BURLEY-IN-
WHARFDALE

CLITHEROE

STEETON & SILSDEN

KEIGHLEY

CROSSFLATTS

WHALLEY

LANGHO

ROSE
GROVE

COLNE

NELSON

INGROW WEST
DAMENS
OAKWORTH
HAWORTH
OXENHOPE

SHIPLEY

KIRKHAM &
WESHAM

SALWICK

RAMSGREAVE &
WILPSHIRE

PADIHAM

HAPTON

BRIERFIELD

BURNLEY CENTRAL

(T)

KEIGHLEY & WORTH
VALLEY RAILWAY

BRADFORD

MOSS
SIDE

DEEPDALE

DOCKS

RISHTON

BURNLEY BARRACKS

BURNLEY
MANCHESTER ROAD

See p.42

LYTHAM

PRESTON

BLACKBURN

HUNCOAT

ACCRINGTON

MYTHOLMROYD

SOWERBY
BRIDGE

LOSTOCK
HALL

PLEASINGTON

CHURCH &
OSWALDTWISTLE

HALIFAX

BAMBER
BRIDGE

CHERRY
TREE

MILL HILL

TODMORDEN

HEBDEN
BRIDGE

See p.42

20A3

20B3

M 15 10 5 0 5 10 15 20 Km

**15**

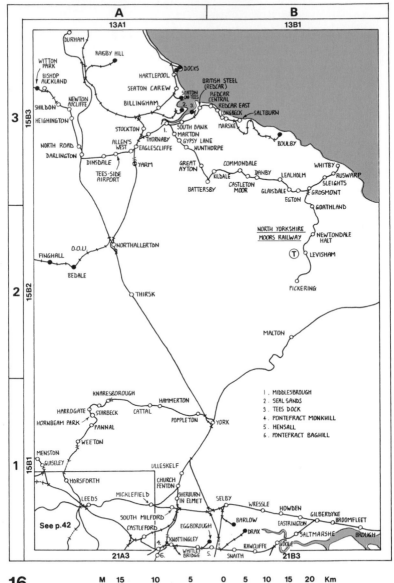

See p.42

**16**

M   15      10      5      0      5      10      15      20   Km

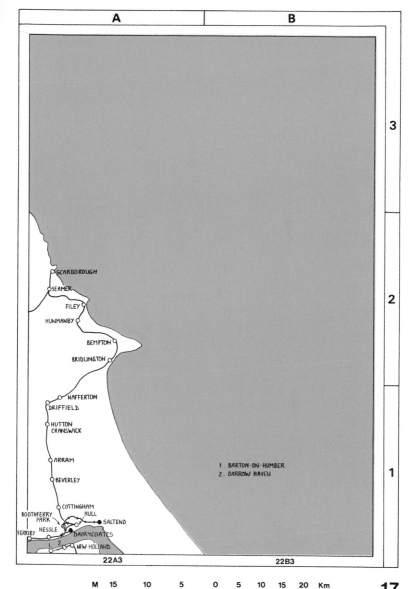

3

2

1

SCARBOROUGH
SEAMER
FILEY
HUNMANBY
BEMPTON
BRIDLINGTON
NAFFERTON
DRIFFIELD
HUTTON CRANSWICK
ARRAM
BEVERLEY
COTTINGHAM
BOOTHFERRY PARK
HULL
SALTEND
FERRIBY
HESSLE
DAIRYCOATES
NEW HOLLAND

1. BARTON-ON-HUMBER
2. BARROW HAVEN

M  15    10    5    0    5    10    15    20  Km

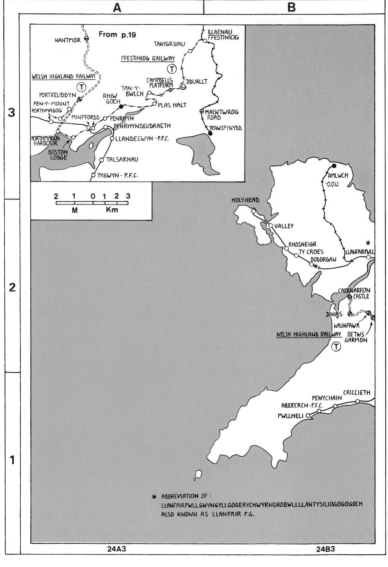

From p.19

NANTMOR

GLAENAU
FFESTINIOG

TANYGRSIAU

FFESTINIOG RAILWAY

WELSH HIGHLAND RAILWAY (T)

CAMPBELL'S
PLATFORM

DDUALLT

PORTREUDDYN

TAN-Y-
BWLCH

PEN-Y-MOUNT

RHIW
GOCH

PLAS HALT

PORTHMADOG

MINFFORDD

PENRHYN

MAENTWROG
ROAD

PENRHYNDEUDRAETH

PORTHMADOG
HARBOUR

TRAWSFYNYDD

LLANDECWYN - P.F.C.

BOSTON
LODGE

TALSARNAU

TYGWYN - P.F.C.

2  1  0  1  2  3
M        Km

AMLWCH
-O.O.U.

HOLYHEAD

VALLEY

RHOSNEIGR
TY CROES
BODORGAN

LLANFAIRPWLL *

CAERNARFON
CASTLE

DINAS

WAUNFAWR

WELSH HIGHLAND RAILWAY

BETWS
GARMON

(T)

CRICCIETH

PENYCHAIN

ABERERCH - P.F.C.

PWLLHELI

* ABBREVIATION OF :
LLANFAIRPWLLGWYNGYLLGOGERYCHWYRNDROBWLLLLANTYSILIOGOGOGOCH
ALSO KNOWN AS LLANFAIR P.G.

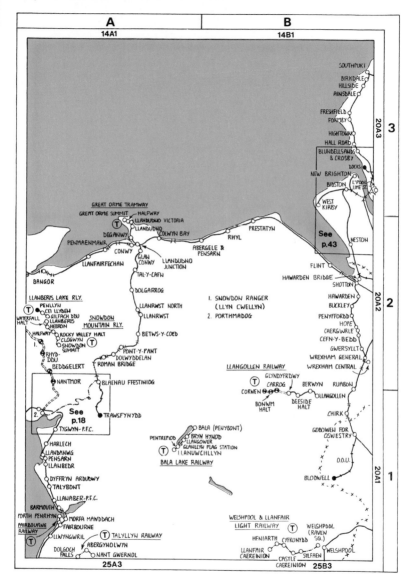

| | A | | B | |
|---|---|---|---|---|
| | 14A1 | | 14B1 | |

SOUTHPORT
BIRKDALE
HILLSIDE
AINSDALE

FRESHFIELD
FORMBY

HIGHTOWN
HALL ROAD
BLUNDELLSANDS
& CROSBY
DOCKS
NEW BRIGHTON
BIDSTON        L'POOL
                LIME ST.
WEST
KIRBY
                NESTON

**3**

**20A3**

See
p.43

**GREAT ORME TRAMWAY**
GREAT ORME SUMMIT — HALFWAY
LLANDUDNO VICTORIA
LLANDUDNO
DEGANWY      COLWYN BAY      PRESTATYN
PENMAENMAWR                  RHYL
CONWY
GLAN
LLANFAIRFECHAN   CONWY   LLANDUDNO
              TAL-Y-CAFN   JUNCTION   ABERGELE &
                                      PENSARN
BANGOR
                                      FLINT
              DOLGARROG              HAWARDEN BRIDGE
                                      SHOTTON
**LLANBERIS LAKE RLY.**            HAWARDEN
    PENLLYN    LLANRWST NORTH      BUCKLEY
CEI LLYDAN  LLANRWST
WATERFALL  GILFACH DDU             PENYFFORDD
HALT   LLANBERIS   **SNOWDON**      HOPE
       HEBRON     **MOUNTAIN RLY.** CAERGWRLE
HALFWAY  ROCKY VALLEY HALT  BETWS-Y-COED  CEFN-Y-BEDD
    CLOGWYN                          GWERSYLLT
    SNOWDON                         WREXHAM GENERAL
RHYD  SUMMIT                        WREXHAM CENTRAL
DDU        PONT-Y-PANT
BEDDGELERT  DOLWYDDELAN
           ROMAN BRIDGE   **LLANGOLLEN RAILWAY**
  NANTMOR                      GLYNDYFRDWY
           BLAENAU FFESTINIOG    CARROG   BERWYN   RUABON
See                        CORWEN            LLANGOLLEN
p.18                              DEESIDE
                          BONWM    HALT
      TRAWSFYNYDD          HALT
                                          CHIRK
TYGWYN - P.F.C.
                                     GOBOWEN FOR
HARLECH        BALA (PENYBONT)        OSWESTRY
LLANDANWG   PENTREPIOD  BRYN HYNOD
PENSARN              LLANGOWER        D.D.U.
LLANBEDR          GLANLLYN FLAG STATION
DYFFRYN ARDUDWY    LLANUWCHLLYN      BLODWELL
TALYBONT          **BALA LAKE RAILWAY**
LLANABER - P.F.C.
BARMOUTH
PORTH PENRHYN
**FAIRBOURNE**   MORFA MAWDDACH   **WELSHPOOL & LLANFAIR**
**RAILWAY**  FAIRBOURNE         **LIGHT RAILWAY**   WELSHPOOL
LLWYNGWRIL   **TALYLLYN RAILWAY**              (RAVEN
           ABERGYNOLWYN       HENIARTH  CYFRONYDD  SQ.)
DOLGOCH                   LLANFAIR            WELSHPOOL
FALLS    NANT GWERNOL     CAEREINION  CASTLE  SYLFAEN
                                    CAEREINION

1. SNOWDON RANGER
   (LLYN CWELLYN)
2. PORTHMADOG

**20A2**

**20A1**

| 25A3 | | 25B3 | |
|---|---|---|---|

M   15   10   5   0   5   10   15   20  Km

**19**

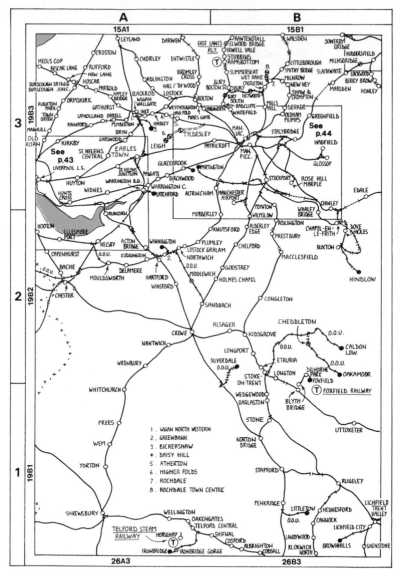

A | B

15A1 | 15B1

3

19B3

LEYLAND
DARWEN
EAST LANCS.
RLY.
RAWTENSTALL
ELWOOD BRIDGE
IRWELL VALE
STUBBINS
RAMSBOTTOM
WALSDEN
SOWERBY
BRIDGE
HUDDERSFIELD
MILNSBRIDGE
MEOLS COP
BESCAR LANE
CROSTON
CHORLEY
ENTWISTLE
BROMLEY
CROSS
SUMMERSEAT
WET RAKE
CASTLETON
LITTLEBOROUGH
SMITHY BRIDGE
MILNROW
NEW HEY
SHAW &
CROMPTON
SLAITHWAITE
LOCKWOOD
BERRY BROW
HONLEY
MARSDEN
RUFFORD
NEW LANE
HOSCAR
PARBOLD
ADLINGTON
HALL I' TH'WOOD
LOSTOCK
BOLTON
BURY
BOLTON ST.
BURY
SOUTH
HEYWOOD
RADCLIFFE
WHITEFIELD
MILLS
HILL
DERKER
OLDHAM
MUMPS
GREENFIELD
BURSCOUGH BRIDGE
BURSCOUGH JUNC.
ORMSKIRK
GATHURST
APPLEY
BRIDGE
BLACKROD
WIGAN
WALLGATE
INCE
AUGHTON
PARK
UPHOLLAND
ORRELL
RAINFORD
PEMBERTON
BRYN
HINDLEY
WESTHOUGHTON
HAG FOLD
MOSES GATE
FARNWORTH
MAN.
VIC.
STALYBRIDGE
See
p.44
HADFIELD
GLOSSOP
TOWN
GREEN
MAGHULL
OLD
ROAN
KIRKBY
See
p.43
GARSWOOD
EARLES
TOWN
TYLDESLEY
LEIGH
PATRICROFT
MAN.
PICC.
ST.HELENS
CENTRAL
LIVERPOOL L.S.
HUYTON
GLAZEBROOK
PARTINGTON
ST.HELENS
JUNCTION
BIRCHWOOD
WARRINGTON B.Q.
WARRINGTON C.
MANCHESTER
AIRPORT
STOCKPORT
ROSE HILL
MARPLE
PADGATE
ALTRINCHAM
HUNTS
CROSS
WIDNES
LATCHFORD
MOBBERLEY
POYNTON
WILMSLOW
WHALEY
BRIDGE
CHINLEY
EDALE
RUNCORN
KNUTSFORD
ALDERLEY
EDGE
PRESTBURY
ADLINGTON
CHAPEL-EN-
LE-FRITH
DOVE
HOLES
BUXTON

2

19B2

HOOTON
ELLESMERE
PORT
HELSBY
ACTON
BRIDGE
D.O.U.
CUDDINGTON
WINNINGTON
PLUMLEY
LOSTOCK GRALAM
NORTHWICH
CHELFORD
MACCLESFIELD
HINDLOW
CAPENHURST
BACHE
D.O.U.
DELAMERE
MOULDSWORTH
HARTFORD
WINSFORD
MIDDLEWICH
D.O.U.
GOOSTREY
HOLMES CHAPEL
CHESTER
SANDBACH
CONGLETON
ALSAGER
CHEDDLETON
CREWE
KIDSGROVE
D.O.U.
CALDON
LOW
NANTWICH
LONGPORT
ETRURIA
D.O.U.
OAKAMOOR
WRENBURY
SILVERDALE
D.O.U.
STOKE-
ON-TRENT
LONGTON
DILHORNE
PARK
FOXFIELD
WHITCHURCH
WEDGEWOOD
BARLASTON
BLYTHE
BRIDGE
FOXFIELD RAILWAY
PREES
STONE
UTTOXETER

1

19B1

WEM
YORTON
1. WIGAN NORTH WESTERN
2. GREENBANK
3. BICKERSHAW
4. DAISY HILL
5. ATHERTON
6. HIGHER FOLDS
7. ROCHDALE
8. ROCHDALE TOWN CENTRE
NORTON
BRIDGE
STAFFORD
RUGELEY
PENKRIDGE
LITTLETON
D.O.U.
HEDNESFORD
CANNOCK
LICHFIELD
TRENT
VALLEY
SHREWSBURY
WELLINGTON
OAKENGATES
TELFORD CENTRAL
LANDYWOOD
BLOXWICH
NORTH
LICHFIELD CITY
TELFORD STEAM
RAILWAY
HORSEHAY
SHIFNAL
COSFORD
ALBRIGHTON
CODSALL
BROWNHILLS
SHENSTONE
IRONBRIDGE
IRONBRIDGE GORGE

26A3 | 26B3

20

M 15 10 5 0 5 10 15 20 Km

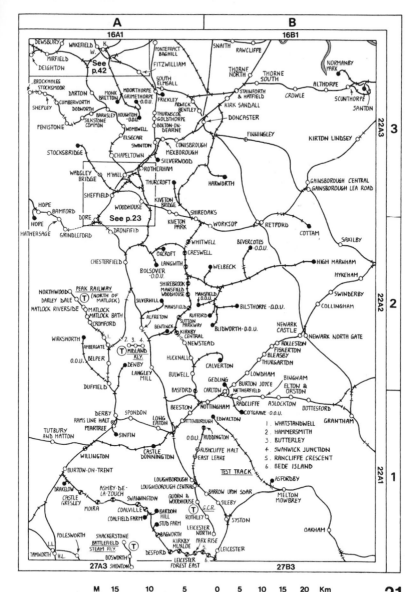

See p.42

See p.23

1. WHATSTANDWELL
2. HAMMERSMITH
3. BUTTERLEY
4. SWANWICK JUNCTION
5. RANCLIFFE CRESCENT
6. BEDE ISLAND

TEST TRACK

PEAK RAILWAY (NORTH OF MATLOCK)

MIDLAND RLY.

BATTLEFIELD STEAM RLY.

G.C.R.

M   15   10   5   0   5   10   15   20   Km

21

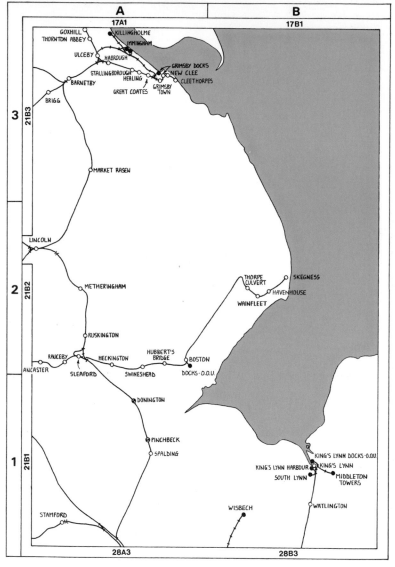

GOXHILL
THORNTON ABBEY
KILLINGHOLME
IMMINGHAM
ULCEBY
HABROUGH
STALLINGBOROUGH
HEALING
GRIMSBY DOCKS
NEW CLEE
CLEETHORPES
BARNETBY
GREAT COATES
GRIMSBY TOWN
BRIGG

MARKET RASEN

LINCOLN

METHERINGHAM
THORPE CULVERT
SKEGNESS
HAVENHOUSE
WAINFLEET

RUSKINGTON

RAUCEBY
HECKINGTON
HUBBERT'S BRIDGE
BOSTON
ANCASTER
SLEAFORD
SWINESHEAD
DOCKS-D.O.U.

DONINGTON

PINCHBECK

SPALDING
KING'S LYNN DOCKS-D.O.U.
KING'S LYNN HARBOUR
KING'S LYNN
SOUTH LYNN
MIDDLETON TOWERS

WATLINGTON

STAMFORD
WISBECH

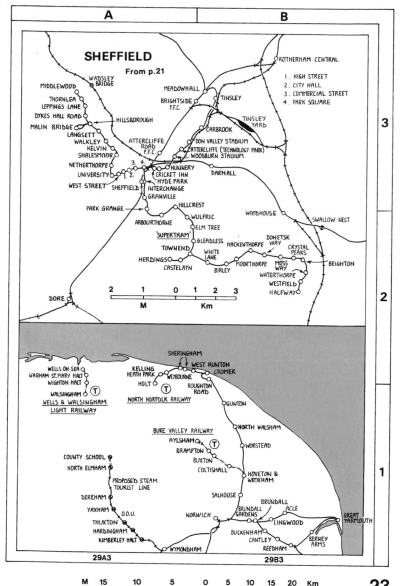

SHEFFIELD
From p.21

A

MIDDLEWOOD
WADSLEY BRIDGE
THORNLEA
LEPPINGS LANE
DYKES HALL ROAD
MALIN BRIDGE
HILLSBOROUGH
LANGSETT
WALKLEY
KELVIN
SHALESMOOR
NETHERTHORPE
UNIVERSITY
WEST STREET
SHEFFIELD INTERCHANGE
ATTERCLIFFE ROAD P.F.C.
3. 4.
1. 2.
NUNNERY
CRICKET INN
HYDE PARK
GRANVILLE
HILLCREST
PARK GRANGE
ARBOURTHORNE
WULFRIC
ELM TREE
'SUPERTRAM'
TOWNEND
GLEADLESS
WHITE LANE
HERDINGS
CASTELAYN
BIRLEY
MOORTHORPE
HACKENTHORPE
DONETSK WAY
CRYSTAL PEAKS
MOSS WAY
WATERTHORPE
WESTFIELD
HALFWAY
BEIGHTON

DORE

B

ROTHERHAM CENTRAL

1. HIGH STREET
2. CITY HALL
3. COMMERCIAL STREET
4. PARK SQUARE

MEADOWHALL
BRIGHTSIDE P.F.C.
TINSLEY
CARBROOK
TINSLEY YARD
DON VALLEY STADIUM
ATTERCLIFFE (TECHNOLOGY PARK)
WOODBURN STADIUM
DARNALL

WOODHOUSE
SWALLOW NEST

2   1   0   1   2   3
M        Km

3

2

SHERINGHAM
WEST RUNTON
CROMER
KELLING HEATH PARK
WEYBOURNE
HOLT
ROUGHTON ROAD
GUNTON
NORTH NORFOLK RAILWAY

WELLS-ON-SEA
WARHAM ST.MARY HALT
WIGHTON HALT
WALSINGHAM (T)
WELLS & WALSINGHAM LIGHT RAILWAY

NORTH WALSHAM

BURE VALLEY RAILWAY
AYLSHAM (T)
BRAMPTON
BUXTON
COLTISHALL
WORSTEAD
HOVETON & WROXHAM

COUNTY SCHOOL
NORTH ELMHAM
PROPOSED STEAM TOURIST LINE
DEREHAM
YAXHAM
D.D.U.
THUXTON
HARDINGHAM
KIMBERLEY HALT
WYMONDHAM

SALHOUSE
NORWICH
BUCKENHAM
CANTLEY
REEDHAM

BRUNDALL GARDENS
BRUNDALL
ACLE
LINGWOOD
BERNEY ARMS
GREAT YARMOUTH

1

29A3                                    29B3

M   15    10    5    0    5    10    15    20   Km

23

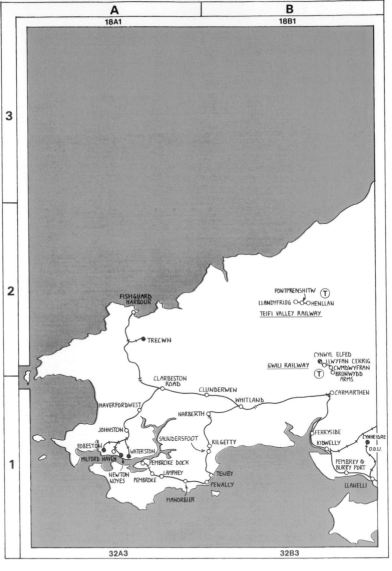

3

2

PONTPRENSHITW Ⓣ
LLANDYFRIOG ○─○○HENLLAN
**TEIFI VALLEY RAILWAY**

CYNWYL ELFED
○ LLWYFAN CERRIG
**GWILI RAILWAY** ○ CWMDWYFRAN
○ BRONWYDD
Ⓣ ARMS

FISHGUARD
HARBOUR

TRECWN

○ CARMARTHEN

CLARBESTON
ROAD
○
CLUNDERWEN
○ WHITLAND
HAVERFORDWEST
○ NARBERTH
○
JOHNSTON ○
SAUNDERSFOOT FERRYSIDE ○
ROBESTON ○ KILGETTY ○ ○ KIDWELLY ○ CYNHEIDRE
WATERSTON ○ D.O.U.
MILFORD HAVEN ● PEMBROKE DOCK
○ PEMBREY &
NEWTON LAMPHEY BURRY PORT
NOYES ○ PEMBROKE ○ TENBY
○ ○ PENALLY LLANELLI
MANORBIER

1

**24**   M 15 10 5 0 5 10 15 20 Km

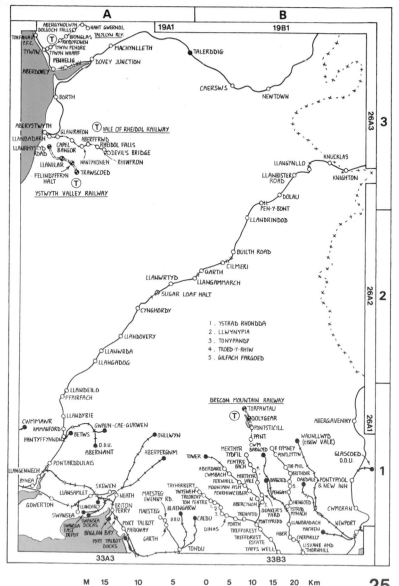

TONFANAU
P.F.C.
ABERGYNOLWYN
DOLGOCH FALLS
NANT GWERNOL
TALYLLYN RLY.
BRONGLAS
RHYDYRONEN
TYWYN
TYWYN PENDRE
TYWYN WHARF
PENHELIG
MACHYNLLETH
TALERDDIG
ABERDOVEY
DOVEY JUNCTION
CAERSWS
NEWTOWN
BORTH

ABERYSTWYTH
GLANRAFON
VALE OF RHEIDOL RAILWAY
KNUCKLAS
LLANBADARN
ABERFFRWD
RHEIDOL FALLS
DEVIL'S BRIDGE
RHIWFRON
LLANGYNLLO
KNIGHTON
LLANRHYSTYD
ROAD
CAPEL
BANGOR
LLANBISTER
ROAD
LLANILAR
NANTYRONEN
TRAWSCOED
DOLAU
FELINDYFFRYN
HALT
PEN-Y-BONT

YSTWYTH VALLEY RAILWAY
LLANDRINDOD

BUILTH ROAD

CILMERI
GARTH
LLANWRTYD
LLANGAMMARCH

SUGAR LOAF HALT

CYNGHORDY

1 . YSTRAD RHONDDA
2 . LLWYNYPIA
3 . TONYPANDY
4 . TROED-Y-RHIW
5 . GILFACH FARGOED

LLANDOVERY

LLANWRDA
LLANGADOG

LLANDEILO
FFAIRFACH

BRECON MOUNTAIN RAILWAY

LLANDYBIE
TORPANTAU
DOLYGEAR
PONTSTICILL
ABERGAVENNY
CWMMAWR
AMMANFORD
GWAUN-CAE-GURWEN
PANT
WAUNLLWYD
(EBBW VALE)
PANTYFFYNNON
BETWS
MERTHYR
TYDFIL
CWM
BARGOED
R.TYMNEY
PONTLOTTYN
GLASCOED
D.D.U.
ABERNANT
ONLLWYN
ABERPERGWM
TOWER
PENTRE
BACH
TIR-PHIL
BRITHDIR
OAKDALE
PONTYPOOL
& NEW INN
LLANGENNECH
PONTARDDULAIS
ABERDARE
CWMBACH
FERNHILL
MERTHYR
VALE
BARGOED
PENGAM
HENGOED
BYNEA
SKEWEN
TREHERBERT
TYNYSWEN
TREORCHY
MOUNTAIN ASH
PENRHIWCEIBER
QUAKER'S
YARD
YSTRAD
MYNACH
CWMBRAN
LLANSAMLET
NEATH
MAESTEG
EWENNY RD.
TON PENTRE
N.
ABERCYNON
GOWERTON
LLANDARCY
MAESTEG
BLAENGARW
PORTH
PONTYPRIDD
LLANBRADACH
MACHEN
NEWPORT
SWANSEA
BRITON
FERRY
TREHAFOD
ABER
CAERPHILLY
SWANSEA DOCKS
SWANSEA
EAST DEPOT
CAEDU
DINAS
TREFFOREST
ESTATE
LISVANE AND
THORNHILL
PORT TALBOT
PARKWAY
PORT TALBOT
DOCKS
BAGLAN BAY
GARTH
TONDU
TREFFOREST
TAFFS WELL

M    15        10        5        0        5        10        15        20   Km

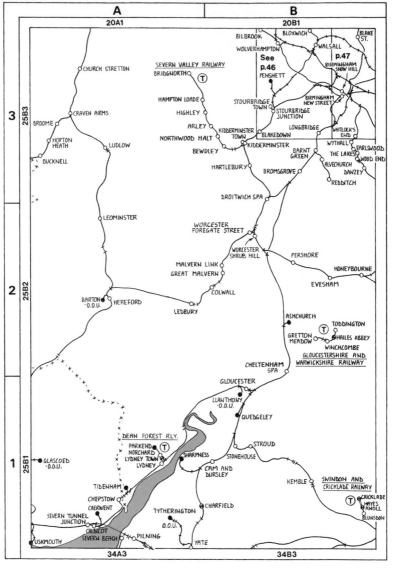

A                                    B

20A1                               20B1

BILBROOK
BLOXWICH                    BLAKE
ST.
WOLVERHAMPTON          WALSALL
See
p.46        p.47
BIRMINGHAM
SNOW HILL
PENSHETT

SEVERN VALLEY RAILWAY
BRIDGNORTH                        T

CHURCH STRETTON

3  HAMPTON LOADE                STOURBRIDGE
TOWN
HIGHLEY                       STOURBRIDGE     BIRMINGHAM
JUNCTION    NEW STREET
CRAVEN ARMS          ARLEY       KIDDERMINSTER      LONGBRIDGE
BROOME                        NORTHWOOD HALT    TOWN                        WHITLOCK'S
BLAKEDOWN                 END
HOPTON                     BEWDLEY       KIDDERMINSTER   WYTHALL    EARLSWOOD
HEATH      LUDLOW                                    BARNT          THE LAKES  WOOD END
BUCKNELL                    HARTLEBURY    GREEN        ALVECHURCH
DANZEY
BROMSGROVE            REDDITCH

DROITWICH SPA

LEOMINSTER
WORCESTER
FOREGATE STREET
WORCESTER
SHRUB HILL       PERSHORE
MALVERN LINK
GREAT MALVERN                        HONEYBOURNE
2                                 COLWALL           EVESHAM
BARTON
-D.O.U.  HEREFORD                LEDBURY
ASHCHURCH
TODDINGTON
GRETTON    T  HAILES ABBEY
MEADOW    WINCHCOMBE
GLOUCESTERSHIRE AND
WARWICKSHIRE RAILWAY
CHELTENHAM
SPA
GLOUCESTER
LLANTHONY
-D.O.U.
QUEDGELEY

DEAN FOREST RLY.             STROUD
PARKEND
GLASCOED        NORCHARD    T
1   -D.O.U.        LYDNEY TOWN      SHARPNESS   STONEHOUSE
LYDNEY
CAM AND
TIDENHAM                 DURSLEY       KEMBLE     SWINDON AND
CHEPSTOW                                 CRICKLADE RAILWAY
CAERWENT                           CRICKLADE
SEVERN TUNNEL             TYTHERINGTON    CHARFIELD            HAYES  T
JUNCTION                                           KNOLL
CALDICOT                              BLUNSDON
USKMOUTH  SEVERN BEACH  PILNING      D.O.U.
YATE

34A3                               34B3

26                M  15    10    5    0    5    10   15   20  Km

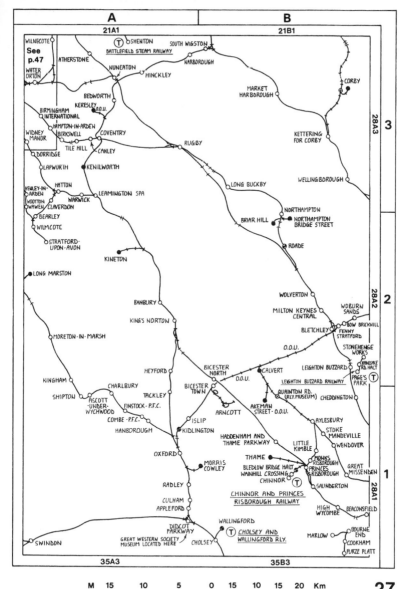

WILNECOTE
See p.47
ATHERSTONE
WATER ORTON

SHENTON
(T) Battlefield Steam Railway
SOUTH WIGSTON
NUNEATON
NARBOROUGH
HINCKLEY
CORBY

MARKET HARBOROUGH

BEDWORTH
KERESLEY O.D.U.
BIRMINGHAM INTERNATIONAL
HAMPTON-IN-ARDEN
WIDNEY MANOR
BERKSWELL
COVENTRY
TILE HILL
CANLEY
DORRIDGE
LAPWORTH
KENILWORTH
RUGBY
LONG BUCKBY
KETTERING FOR CORBY
WELLINGBOROUGH

HENLEY-IN-ARDEN
WOOTTON WAWEN
CLAVERDON
HATTON
WARWICK
LEAMINGTON SPA
NORTHAMPTON
BRIAR HILL
NORTHAMPTON BRIDGE STREET
BEARLEY
WILMCOTE
STRATFORD-UPON-AVON
ROADE

LONG MARSTON
KINETON

WOLVERTON
WOBURN SANDS
BANBURY
MILTON KEYNES CENTRAL
BOW BRICKHILL
KING'S NORTON
BLETCHLEY
FENNY STRATFORD
MORETON-IN-MARSH
O.D.U.
STONEHENGE WORKS
HEYFORD
BICESTER NORTH
CALVERT
LEIGHTON BUZZARD
WYNDYKE FARM HALT
KINGHAM
CHARLBURY
TACKLEY
BICESTER TOWN
D.O.U.
LEIGHTON BUZZARD RAILWAY
PAGE'S PARK (T)
SHIPTON
ASCOTT-UNDER-WYCHWOOD
FINSTOCK-P.F.C.
QUAINTON RD. (RLY.MUSEUM)
CHEDDINGTON
COMBE-P.F.C.
ARNCOTT
AKEMAN STREET-O.D.U.
HANBOROUGH
ISLIP
KIDLINGTON
AYLESBURY
STOKE MANDEVILLE
OXFORD
HADDENHAM AND THAME PARKWAY
LITTLE KIMBLE
WENDOVER
MORRIS COWLEY
THAME
MONKS RISBOROUGH
RADLEY
BLEDLOW BRIDGE HALT
WAINHILL CROSSING
PRINCES RISBOROUGH
GREAT MISSENDEN
CHINNOR (T)
SAUNDERTON
CULHAM
CHINNOR AND PRINCES RISBOROUGH RAILWAY
HIGH WYCOMBE
BEACONSFIELD
APPLEFORD
WALLINGFORD
DIDCOT PARKWAY (T) CHOLSEY AND WALLINGFORD RLY.
SWINDON
GREAT WESTERN SOCIETY MUSEUM LOCATED HERE
CHOLSEY
MARLOW
BOURNE END
COOKHAM
FURZE PLATT

M 15 10 5 0 15 10 15 20 Km

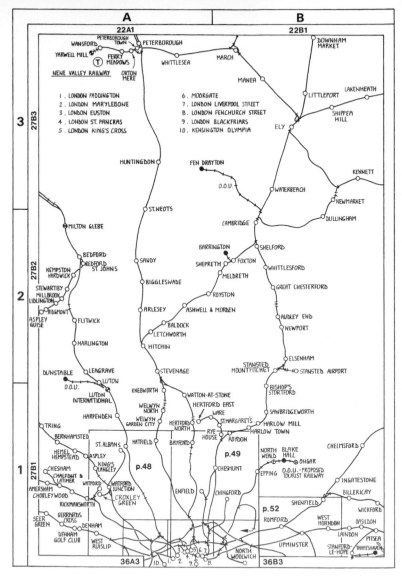

| | A | | B | |
|---|---|---|---|---|

22A1 · 22B1

PETERBOROUGH
WANSFORD · PETERBOROUGH TOWN
YARWELL MILL · FERRY MEADOWS (T)
NENE VALLEY RAILWAY · OKTON MERE
WHITTLESEA · MARCH · MANEA
DOWNHAM MARKET
LITTLEPORT · LAKENHEATH
SHIPPEA HILL
ELY

1. LONDON PADDINGTON
2. LONDON MARYLEBONE
3. LONDON EUSTON
4. LONDON ST. PANCRAS
5. LONDON KING'S CROSS
6. MOORGATE
7. LONDON LIVERPOOL STREET
8. LONDON FENCHURCH STREET
9. LONDON BLACKFRIARS
10. KENSINGTON OLYMPIA

HUNTINGDON · FEN DRAYTON
O.O.U. · WATERBEACH · KENNETT
ST. NEOTS · CAMBRIDGE · NEWMARKET · DULLINGHAM
MILTON GLEBE
BEDFORD · SANDY · BARRINGTON · SHELFORD
KEMPSTON HARDWICK · BEDFORD ST. JOHNS · SHEPRETH · FOXTON · WHITTLESFORD
STEWARTBY · BIGGLESWADE · MELDRETH · GREAT CHESTERFORD
MILLBROOK · LIDLINGTON · RIDGMONT · ROYSTON
ASPLEY GUISE · FLITWICK · ARLESEY · ASHWELL & MORDEN · AUDLEY END
HARLINGTON · BALDOCK · NEWPORT
LETCHWORTH
DUNSTABLE · LEAGRAVE · HITCHIN · ELSENHAM
O.O.U. · LUTON · STEVENAGE · STANSTED MOUNTFITCHET · STANSTED AIRPORT
LUTON INTERNATIONAL · KNEBWORTH · WATTON-AT-STONE · BISHOP'S STORTFORD
HARPENDEN · WELWYN NORTH · HERTFORD EAST · WARE · SAWBRIDGEWORTH
TRING · WELWYN GARDEN CITY · HERTFORD NORTH · ST.MARGARET'S · HARLOW MILL
BERKHAMSTED · RYE HOUSE · HARLOW TOWN
HEMEL HEMPSTEAD · ST. ALBANS · HATFIELD · BAYFORD · ROYDON · CHELMSFORD
ASPLEY · p.48 · p.49 · NORTH WEALD · BLAKE HALL
CHESHAM · KING'S LANGLEY · CHESHUNT · EPPING · ONGAR
CHALFONT & LATIMER · WATFORD · WATFORD JUNCTION · O.O.U.-PROPOSED TOURIST RAILWAY · INGATESTONE
AMERSHAM · CHORLEYWOOD · CROXLEY GREEN · ENFIELD · CHINGFORD · SHENFIELD · BILLERICAY
RICKMANSWORTH · p.52 · WICKFORD
SEER GREEN · GERRARDS CROSS · DENHAM · ROMFORD · WEST HORNDON · BASILDON
DENHAM GOLF CLUB · WEST RUISLIP · NORTH WOOLWICH · UPMINSTER · LAINDON · PITSEA
STANFORD-LE-HOPE · THAMESHAVEN

36A3 · 36B3

27B3 · 27B2 · 27B1

**28**

M 15 10 5 0 5 10 15 20 Km

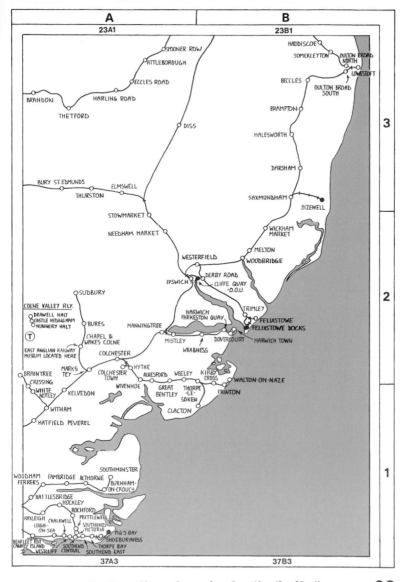

HADDISCOE
SOMERLEYTON
OULTON BROAD NORTH
LOWESTOFT
SPOONER ROW
ATTLEBOROUGH
BECCLES ROAD
BECCLES
OULTON BROAD SOUTH
HARLING ROAD
BRANDON
THETFORD
BRAMPTON
DISS
HALESWORTH
DARSHAM
BURY ST.EDMUNDS
ELMSWELL
THURSTON
SAXMUNDHAM
SIZEWELL
STOWMARKET
WICKHAM MARKET
NEEDHAM MARKET
MELTON
WESTERFIELD
WOODBRIDGE
DERBY ROAD
IPSWICH
CLIFFE QUAY -D.O.U.
SUDBURY
COLNE VALLEY RLY.
DRAWELL HALT
CASTLE HEDINGHAM
NUNNERY HALT
BURES
(T)
CHAPEL & WAKES COLNE
EAST ANGLIAN RAILWAY MUSEUM LOCATED HERE
MANNINGTREE
MISTLEY
WRABNESS
TRIMLEY
HARWICH PARKESTON QUAY
FELIXSTOWE
FELIXSTOWE DOCKS
DOVERCOURT
HARWICH TOWN
COLCHESTER
HYTHE
MARKS TEY
COLCHESTER TOWN
ALRESFORD
WEELEY
KIRBY CROSS
WALTON-ON-NAZE
BRAINTREE
CRESSING
WHITE NOTLEY
KELVEDON
WIVENHOE
GREAT BENTLEY
THORPE-LE-SOKEN
FRINTON
WITHAM
HATFIELD PEVEREL
CLACTON
SOUTHMINSTER
WOODHAM FERRERS
FAMBRIDGE
ALTHORNE
BURNHAM-ON-CROUCH
BATTLESBRIDGE
HOCKLEY
ROCHFORD
RAYLEIGH
CHALKWELL
PRITTLEWELL
LEIGH-ON-SEA
SOUTHEND VICTORIA
PIG'S BAY
SHOEBURYNESS
BENFLEET FOR CANVEY ISLAND
WESTCLIFF
SOUTHEND CENTRAL
THORPE BAY
SOUTHEND EAST

M 15 10 5 0 5 10 15 20 Km

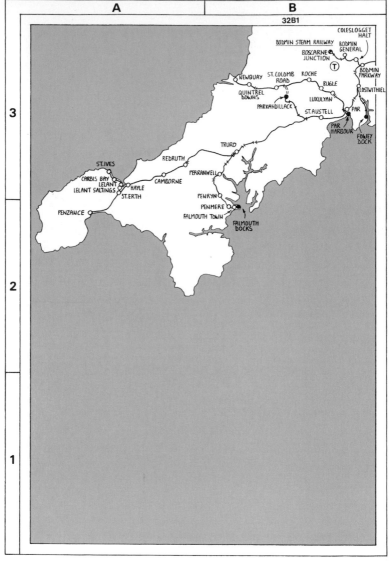

32B1

COLESLOGGET HALT

BODMIN STEAM RAILWAY

BODMIN GENERAL

BOSCARNE JUNCTION

(T)

BODMIN PARKWAY

LOSTWITHIEL

NEWQUAY

ST. COLOMB ROAD

ROCHE

BUGLE

QUINTREL DOWNS

PARKANDILLACK

LUXULYAN

ST. AUSTELL

PAR

PAR HARBOUR

FOWEY DOCK

3

TRURO

REDRUTH

PERRANWELL

ST. IVES

CARBIS BAY

LELANT

CAMBORNE

LELANT SALTINGS

HAYLE

ST. ERTH

PENRYN

PENMERE

FALMOUTH TOWN

FALMOUTH DOCKS

PENZANCE

2

1

30

M   15   10   5   0   5   10   15   20   Km

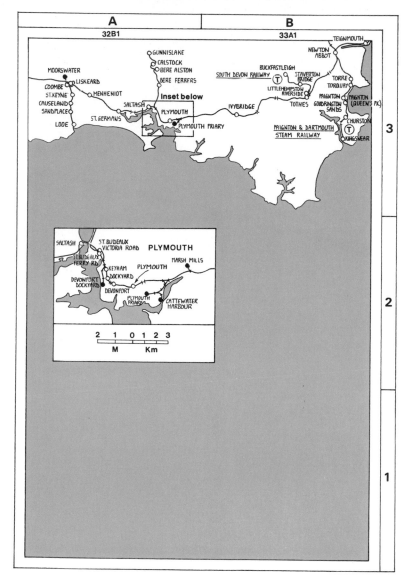

31

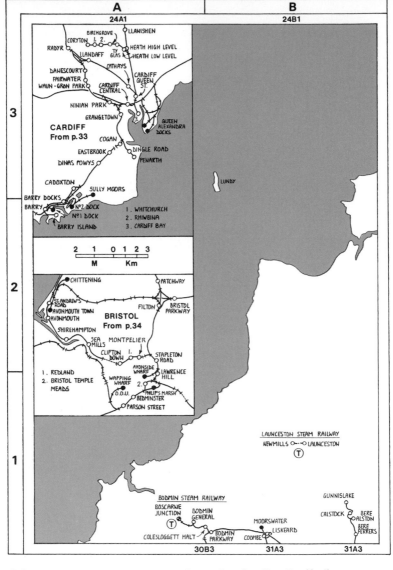

**CARDIFF**
From p.33

LLANISHEN
BIRCHGROVE
CORYTON 1. 2.
RADYR
TY GLAS
HEATH HIGH LEVEL
HEATH LOW LEVEL
LLANDAFF
CATHAYS
DANESCOURT
FAIRWATER
WAUN-GRON PARK
CARDIFF CENTRAL
CARDIFF QUEEN ST.
NINIAN PARK
GRANGETOWN
QUEEN ALEXANDRA DOCKS
COGAN
EASTBROOK
DINGLE ROAD
DINAS POWYS
PENARTH
CADOXTON
SULLY MOORS
BARRY DOCKS
BARRY
Nº2 DOCK
Nº1 DOCK
BARRY ISLAND

1. WHITCHURCH
2. RHIWBINA
3. CARDIFF BAY

LUNDY

2 1 0 1 2 3
M    Km

CHITTENING
PATCHWAY
ST.ANDREW'S ROAD
FILTON
BRISTOL PARKWAY
AVONMOUTH TOWN
AVONMOUTH
**BRISTOL**
From p.34
SHIREHAMPTON
SEA MILLS
MONTPELIER
CLIFTON DOWN 1.
STAPLETON ROAD
AVONSIDE WHARF
LAWRENCE HILL
1. REDLAND
2. BRISTOL TEMPLE MEADS
WAPPING WHARF
2.
O.D.U.
PHILIP'S MARSH
BEDMINSTER
PARSON STREET

LAUNCESTON STEAM RAILWAY
NEWMILLS ○---○ LAUNCESTON
Ⓣ

GUNNISLAKE
BODMIN STEAM RAILWAY
BOSCARNE JUNCTION
BODMIN GENERAL
CALSTOCK
BERE ALSTON
Ⓣ
MOORSWATER
LISKEARD
BERE FERRERS
COLESLOGGETT HALT
BODMIN PARKWAY
COOMBE

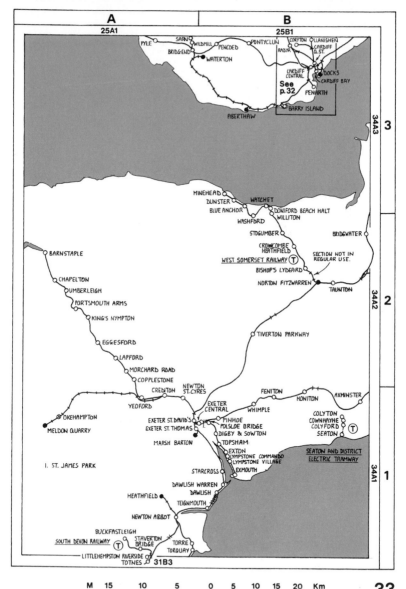

PYLE SARN WILDMILL PENCOED PONTYCLUN CORYTON LLANISHEN
BRIDGEND RADYR CARDIFF Q.ST.
WATERTON CARDIFF CENTRAL DOCKS
CARDIFF BAY
See p. 32 PENARTH
ABERTHAW BARRY ISLAND

MINEHEAD WATCHET
DUNSTER DONIFORD BEACH HALT
BLUE ANCHOR WILLITON
WASHFORD
STOGUMBER BRIDGWATER
CROWCOMBE
HEATHFIELD SECTION NOT IN
WEST SOMERSET RAILWAY (T) REGULAR USE.
BISHOP'S LYDEARD
BARNSTAPLE NORTON FITZWARREN TAUNTON

CHAPELTON
UMBERLEIGH
PORTSMOUTH ARMS
KING'S NYMPTON
EGGESFORD TIVERTON PARKWAY
LAPFORD
MORCHARD ROAD
COPPLESTONE
CREDITON NEWTON FENITON AXMINSTER
ST.CYRES HONITON
YEOFORD EXETER WHIMPLE COLYTON
CENTRAL COWNHAYNE
OKEHAMPTON EXETER ST.DAVID'S PINHOE COLYFORD (T)
MELDON QUARRY EXETER ST.THOMAS POLSLOE BRIDGE SEATON
DIGBY & SOWTON
MARSH BARTON TOPSHAM SEATON AND DISTRICT
EXTON ELECTRIC TRAMWAY
I. ST. JAMES PARK LYMPSTONE COMMANDO
LYMPSTONE VILLAGE
STARCROSS EXMOUTH
DAWLISH WARREN
DAWLISH
HEATHFIELD TEIGNMOUTH

NEWTON ABBOT
BUCKFASTLEIGH
SOUTH DEVON RAILWAY (T) STAVERTON
BRIDGE TORRE
TORQUAY
LITTLEHEMPSTON RIVERSIDE
TOTNES 31B3

M  15   10   5   0   5   10   15   20  Km

**33**

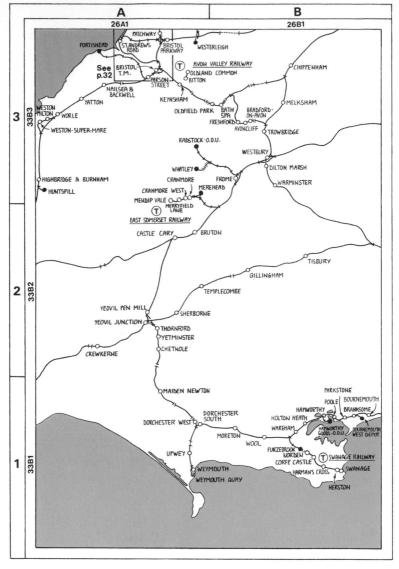

PATCHWAY
PORTISHEAD
ST.ANDREWS ROAD
BRISTOL PARKWAY
WESTERLEIGH
AVON VALLEY RAILWAY
See p.32
BRISTOL T.M.
PARSON STREET
OLDLAND COMMON
BITTON
CHIPPENHAM
NAILSEA & BACKWELL
KEYNSHAM
YATTON
MELKSHAM
WESTON MILTON
OLDFIELD PARK
BATH SPA
BRADFORD-ON-AVON
WORLE
FRESHFORD
WESTON-SUPER-MARE
AVONCLIFF
TROWBRIDGE
WESTBURY
RADSTOCK-O.D.U.
DILTON MARSH
HIGHBRIDGE & BURNHAM
WHATLEY
WARMINSTER
HUNTSPILL
CRANMORE
FROME
CRANMORE WEST
MEREHEAD
MENDIP VALE
MERRYFIELD LANE
EAST SOMERSET RAILWAY
CASTLE CARY
BRUTON
TISBURY
GILLINGHAM
TEMPLECOMBE
YEOVIL PEN MILL
SHERBORNE
YEOVIL JUNCTION
THORNFORD
YETMINSTER
CHETNOLE
CREWKERNE
MAIDEN NEWTON
PARKSTONE
BOURNEMOUTH
POOLE
BRANKSOME
HAMWORTHY
DORCHESTER SOUTH
HOLTON HEATH
DORCHESTER WEST
HAMWORTHY GOODS-O.D.U.
BOURNEMOUTH WEST DEPOT
MORETON
WAREHAM
WOOL
UPWEY
FURZEBROOK
NORDEN
SWANAGE RAILWAY
CORFE CASTLE
WEYMOUTH
HARMAN'S CROSS
SWANAGE
WEYMOUTH QUAY
HERSTON

33B3
33B2
33B1

**34**

M  15  10  5  0  5  10  15  20  Km

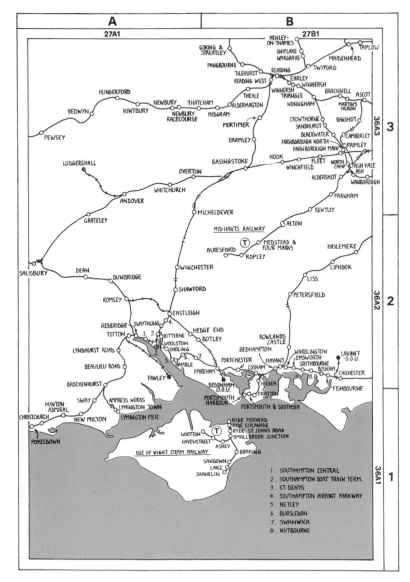

HENLEY-ON-THAMES
TAPLOW
SHIPLAKE
WARGRAVE
MAIDENHEAD
GORING & STREATLEY
TWYFORD
PANGBOURNE
TILEHURST
READING
EARLEY
WINNERSH
WINNERSH TRIANGLE
BRACKNELL
ASCOT
READING WEST
THEALE
HUNGERFORD
NEWBURY
THATCHAM
ALDERMASTON
WOKINGHAM
MARTIN'S HERON
BEDWYN
KINTBURY
NEWBURY RACECOURSE
MIDGHAM
CROWTHORNE
SANDHURST
BAGSHOT
PEWSEY
MORTIMER
BLACKWATER
FARNBOROUGH NORTH
CAMBERLEY
FRIMLEY
BRAMLEY
FARNBOROUGH MAIN
LUDGERSHALL
BASINGSTOKE
HOOK
FLEET
NORTH CAMP
ASH VALE
ASH
OVERTON
WINCHFIELD
ALDERSHOT
WANBOROUGH
WHITCHURCH
ANDOVER
MICHELDEVER
FARNHAM
GRATELEY
BENTLEY
ALTON
MID-HANTS RAILWAY
HASLEMERE
ALRESFORD
MEDSTEAD & FOUR MARKS
SALISBURY
DEAN
DUNBRIDGE
WINCHESTER
ROPLEY
LIPHOOK
LISS
ROMSEY
SHAWFORD
PETERSFIELD
EASTLEIGH
SWAYTHLING
REDBRIDGE
TOTTON
BITTERNE
HEDGE END
BOTLEY
WOOLSTON
SHOLING
ROWLANDS CASTLE
LYNDHURST ROAD
BEDHAMPTON
WARBLINGTON
EMSWORTH
SOUTHBOURNE
BOSHAM
LAVANT -D.O.U.
BEAULIEU ROAD
HAMBLE
PORTCHESTER
HAVANT
CHICHESTER
FAREHAM
COSHAM
FISHBOURNE
FAWLEY
BROCKENHURST
BEDENHAM -D.O.U.
HILSEA
HINTON ADMIRAL
SWAY
AMPRESS WORKS
LYMINGTON TOWN
PORTSMOUTH HARBOUR
FRATTON
CHRISTCHURCH
NEW MILTON
LYMINGTON PIER
PORTSMOUTH & SOUTHSEA
POKESDOWN
RYDE PIERHEAD
RYDE ESPLANADE
RYDE ST JOHNS ROAD
SMALLBROOK JUNCTION
WOOTTON
HAVENSTREET
ASHEY
BRADING
ISLE OF WIGHT STEAM RAILWAY
SANDOWN
LAKE
SHANKLIN

1. SOUTHAMPTON CENTRAL
2. SOUTHAMPTON BOAT TRAIN TERM.
3. ST. DENYS
4. SOUTHAMPTON AIRPORT PARKWAY
5. NETLEY
6. BURSLEDON
7. SWANWICK
8. NUTBOURNE

M  15  10  5  0  5  10  15  20  Km

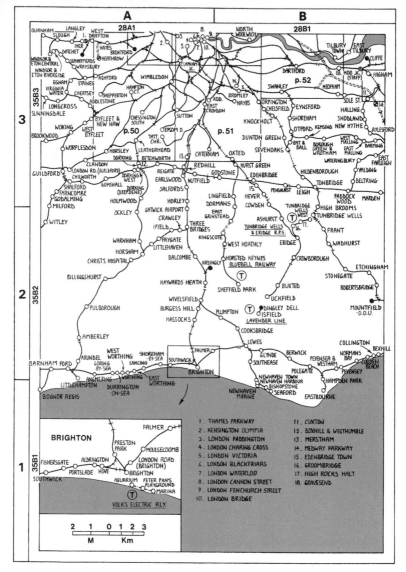

Map legend / index:

| | |
|---|---|
| 1. THAMES PARKWAY | 11. CUXTON |
| 2. KENSINGTON OLYMPIA | 12. BOXHILL & WESTHUMBLE |
| 3. LONDON PADDINGTON | 13. MERSTHAM |
| 4. LONDON CHARING CROSS | 14. MEDWAY PARKWAY |
| 5. LONDON VICTORIA | 15. EDENBRIDGE TOWN |
| 6. LONDON BLACKFRIARS | 16. GROOMBRIDGE |
| 7. LONDON WATERLOO | 17. HIGH ROCKS HALT |
| 8. LONDON CANNON STREET | 18. GRAVESEND |
| 9. LONDON FENCHURCH STREET | |
| 10. LONDON BRIDGE | |

**BRIGHTON**

VOLK'S ELECTRIC RLY.

Scale:
2 1 0 1 2 3
M   Km

**36**

M 15 10 5 0 5 10 15 20 Km

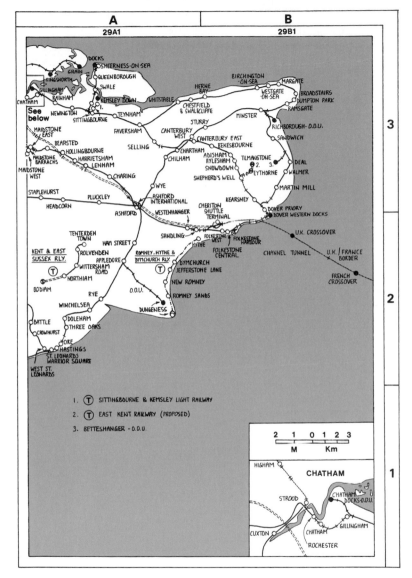

| | A | B |
|---|---|---|
| | 29A1 | 29B1 |

3

DOCKS
SHEERNESS-ON-SEA
GRAIN
KINGSNORTH
QUEENBOROUGH
GILLINGHAM
SWALE
CHATHAM
RAINHAM
KEMSLEY DOWN
See below
NEWINGTON
SITTINGBOURNE
TEYNHAM
WHITSTABLE
HERNE BAY
BIRCHINGTON-ON-SEA
MARGATE
WESTGATE-ON-SEA
BROADSTAIRS
DUMPTON PARK
RAMSGATE
CHESTFIELD & SWALECLIFFE
MAIDSTONE EAST
BEARSTED
FAVERSHAM
STURRY
MINSTER
RICHBOROUGH-D.D.U.
HOLLINGBOURNE
SELLING
CANTERBURY WEST
CANTERBURY EAST
SANDWICH
MAIDSTONE BARRACKS
HARRIETSHAM
CHARTHAM
BEKESBOURNE
TILMANSTONE
DEAL
MAIDSTONE WEST
LENHAM
CHILHAM
ADISHAM
AYLESHAM
2. 3.
EYTHORNE
WALMER
STAPLEHURST
CHARING
SNOWDOWN
SHEPHERD'S WELL
MARTIN MILL
HEADCORN
PLUCKLEY
WYE
ASHFORD INTERNATIONAL
KEARSNEY
DOVER PRIORY
DOVER WESTERN DOCKS
U.K. CROSSOVER
TENTERDEN TOWN
HAM STREET
ASHFORD
WESTENHANGER
CHERITON SHUTTLE TERMINAL
KENT & EAST SUSSEX RLY.
ROLVENDEN
SANDLING
FOLKESTONE WEST
FOLKESTONE CENTRAL
FOLKESTONE HARBOUR
CHANNEL TUNNEL
U.K./FRANCE BORDER
(T)
APPLEDORE
WITTERSHAM ROAD
ROMNEY, HYTHE & DYMCHURCH RLY.
HYTHE
NORTHIAM
(T)
DYMCHURCH
JEFFERSTONE LANE
FRENCH CROSSOVER
BODIAM
O.D.U.
NEW ROMNEY
RYE
ROMNEY SANDS
WINCHELSEA
DUNGENESS
BATTLE
DOLEHAM
THREE OAKS
CROWHURST
ORE
HASTINGS
ST. LEONARDS WARRIOR SQUARE
WEST ST. LEONARDS

1. (T) SITTINGBOURNE & KEMSLEY LIGHT RAILWAY
2. (T) EAST KENT RAILWAY (PROPOSED)
3. BETTESHANGER - O.D.U.

2 1 0 1 2 3
M     Km

HIGHAM
CHATHAM
STROOD
CHATHAM DOCKS-O.D.U.
CUXTON
CHATHAM
GILLINGHAM
ROCHESTER

M   15   10   5   0   5   10   15   20   Km

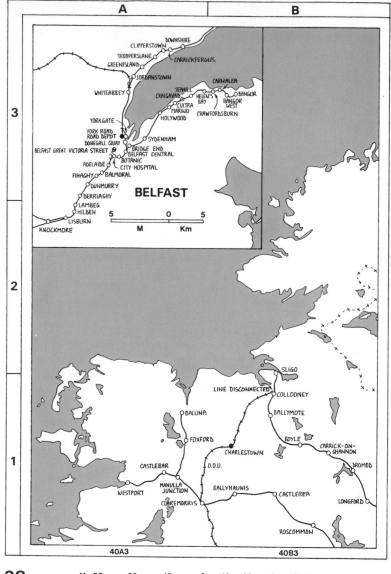

DOWNSHIRE
CLIPPERSTOWN
TROOPERSLANE   CARRICKFERGUS
GREENISLAND
JORDANSTOWN
CARNALEA
WHITEABBEY
SEAHILL   BANGOR
CRAIGAVAD   HELEN'S   BANGOR
CULTRA   BAY   WEST
MARINO   CRAWFORDSBURN
HOLYWOOD
YORKGATE
YORK ROAD
ROAD DEPOT   SYDENHAM
DONEGALL QUAY   BRIDGE END
BELFAST GREAT VICTORIA STREET   BELFAST CENTRAL
BOTANIC
ADELAIDE   CITY HOSPITAL
FINAGHY   BALMORAL
DUNMURRY
DERRIAGHY
LAMBEG
HILDEN
KNOCKMORE   LISBURN

**BELFAST**

5    0    5
M      Km

SLIGO
LINE DISCONNECTED   COLLOONEY
BALLYMOTE
BALLINA
BOYLE
FOXFORD   CARRICK-ON-
CHARLESTOWN   SHANNON
CASTLEBAR   DROMOD
D.D.U.
MANULLA   BALLYHAUNIS
WESTPORT   JUNCTION   CASTLEREA
CLAREMORRIS   LONGFORD
ROSCOMMON

**38**    M 30   20   10   0   10   20   30   40   Km

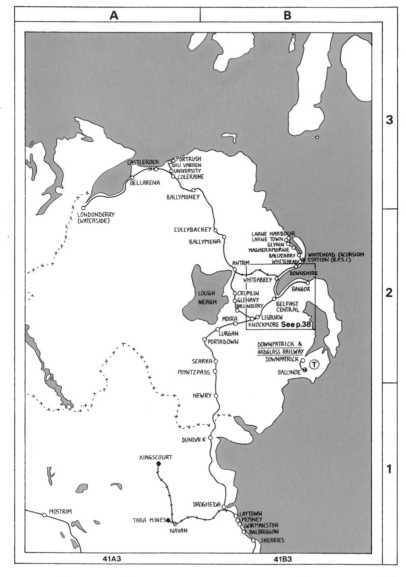

3

PORTRUSH
DHU VARREN
CASTLEROCK
UNIVERSITY
COLERAINE
BELLARENA

BALLYMONEY

LONDONDERRY
(WATERSIDE)

CULLYBACKEY

BALLYMENA

LARNE HARBOUR
LARNE TOWN
GLYNN
MAGHERAMORNE
BALLYCARRY
WHITEHEAD EXCURSION
ANTRIM    WHITEHEAD STATION (R.P.S.I.)

WHITEABBEY    DOWNSHIRE

LOUGH
NEAGH

CRUMLIN
GLENAVY    BANGOR
BALLINDERRY
BELFAST
CENTRAL
MOIRA    LISBURN
KNOCKMORE    **See p.38**

LURGAN

PORTADOWN
DOWNPATRICK &
ARDGLASS RAILWAY
SCARVA
DOWNPATRICK
POYNTZPASS
BALLYNOE   T

NEWRY

2

DUNDALK

KINGSCOURT

MOSTRIM

DROGHEDA
LAYTOWN
MOSNEY
TARA MINES    GORMANSTON
BALBRIGGAN
NAVAN    SKERRIES

1

M 30    20    10    0    10    20    30    40   Km

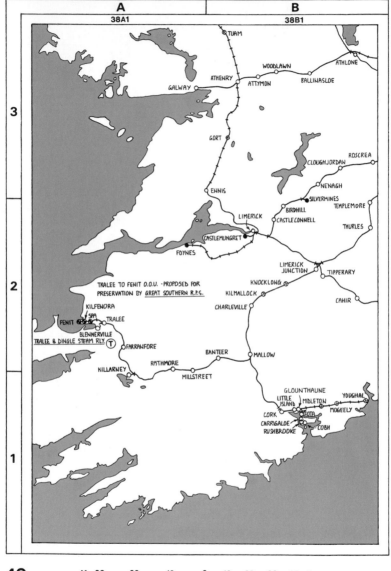

TUAM

WOODLAWN
ATHLONE
ATHENRY ATTYMON BALLINASLOE
GALWAY

3

GORT

ROSCREA
CLOUGHJORDAN
NENAGH
ENNIS SILVERMINES TEMPLEMORE
BIRDHILL
LIMERICK
CASTLECONNELL THURLES
CASTLEMUNGRET
FOYNES

LIMERICK
JUNCTION
TIPPERARY
KNOCKLONG
TRALEE TO FENIT O.O.U. -PROPOSED FOR
PRESERVATION BY GREAT SOUTHERN R.P.S. KILMALLOCK CAHIR
CHARLEVILLE

2

KILFENORA
SPA
FENIT TRALEE
BLENNERVILLE
TRALEE & DINGLE STEAM RLY. (T) FARRANFORE
BANTEER
MALLOW
RATHMORE
KILLARNEY MILLSTREET

GLOUNTHAUNE
LITTLE YOUGHAL
ISLAND MIDLETON
CORK FOTA MOGEELY
CARRIGALDE COBH
RUSHBROOKE

1

M 30 20 10 0 10 20 30 40 Km

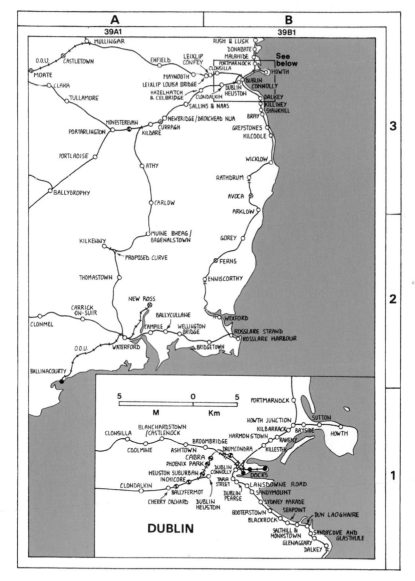

MULLINGAR

O.O.U. CASTLETOWN

MOATE

CLARA

TULLAMORE

ENFIELD

LEIXLIP CONFEY

CLONSILLA

PORTMARNOCK

RUSH & LUSK

DONABATE

MALAHIDE

See below

HOWTH

MAYNOOTH

LEIXLIP LOUISA BRIDGE

HAZELHATCH & CELBRIDGE

CLONDALKIN

DUBLIN HEUSTON

DUBLIN CONNOLLY

SALLINS & NAAS

MONESTEREVAN

CURRAGH

NEWBRIDGE/DROICHEAD NUA

KILDARE

DALKEY

KILLINEY

SHANKHILL

BRAY

PORTARLINGTON

GREYSTONES

KILCOOLE

PORTLAOISE

ATHY

WICKLOW

BALLYBROPHY

RATHDRUM

AVOCA

CARLOW

ARKLOW

KILKENNY

MUINE BHEAG/BAGENALSTOWN

PROPOSED CURVE

GOREY

FERNS

THOMASTOWN

ENNISCORTHY

NEW ROSS

CARRICK-ON-SUIR

BALLYCULLANE

CLONMEL

CAMPILE

WELLINGTON BRIDGE

WEXFORD

ROSSLARE STRAND

ROSSLARE HARBOUR

O.O.U.

WATERFORD

BRIDGETOWN

BALLINACOURTY

3

2

**DUBLIN**

5  0  5
M  Km

PORTMARNOCK

HOWTH JUNCTION

SUTTON

CLONSILLA

BLANCHARDSTOWN/CASTLEKNOCK

BROOMBRIDGE

KILBARRACK

BAYSIDE

HOWTH

HARMONSTOWN

RAHENY

COOLMINE

ASHTOWN

DRUMCONDRA

KILLESTER

CABRA

PHOENIX PARK

HEUSTON SUBURBAN

INCHICORE

DUBLIN CONNOLLY

DOCKS

TARA STREET

LANSDOWNE ROAD

CLONDALKIN

BALLYFERMOT

DUBLIN PEARSE

SANDYMOUNT

CHERRY ORCHARD

DUBLIN HEUSTON

SYDNEY PARADE

BOOTERSTOWN

SEAPOINT

BLACKROCK

DUN LAOGHAIRE

SALTHILL & MONKSTOWN

SANDYCOVE AND GLASTHULE

GLENAGEARY

DALKEY

1

M 30  20  10  0  10  20  30  40  Km

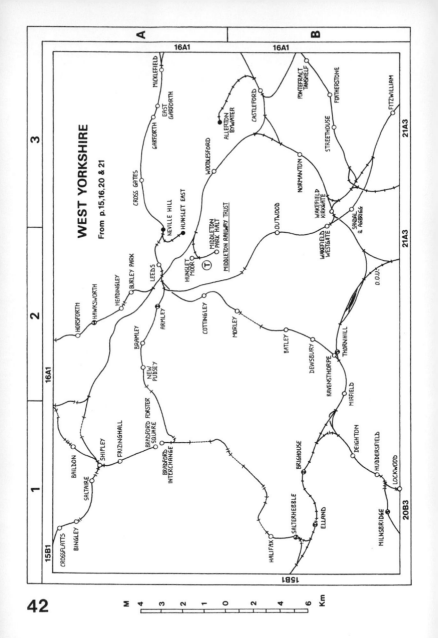

42

# WEST YORKSHIRE

## From p.15,16,20 & 21

MICKLEFIELD
EAST GARFORTH
GARFORTH
CROSS GATES
NEVILLE HILL
HUNSLET EAST
LEEDS
BURLEY PARK
HEADINGLEY
HAWKSWORTH
HORSFORTH
WOODLESFORD
ALLERTON BYWATER
CASTLEFORD
PONTEFRACT TANSHELF
FEATHERSTONE
FITZWILLIAM
STREETHOUSE
NORMANTON
OUTWOOD
WAKEFIELD KIRKGATE
WAKEFIELD WESTGATE
SANDAL & AGBRIGG
(T) MIDDLETON PARK HALT
_MIDDLETON RAILWAY TRUST_
HUNSLET MOOR
ARMLEY
COTTINGLEY
MORLEY
BATLEY
DEWSBURY
RAVENSTHORPE
THORNHILL
MIRFIELD
DEIGHTON
HUDDERSFIELD
LOCKWOOD
MILNSBRIDGE
BRAMLEY
NEW PUDSEY
BRADFORD FOXSTER SQUARE
FRIZINGHALL
SHIPLEY
SALTAIRE
BALDON
BINGLEY
CROSSFLATTS
BRADFORD INTERCHANGE
HALIFAX
SALTERHEBBLE
ELLAND
BRIGHOUSE

16A1
16A1
21A3
21A3
20B3
15B1
15B1
16A1

A
B
3
2
1

M 4
3
2
1
0
1
2
4
Km 6

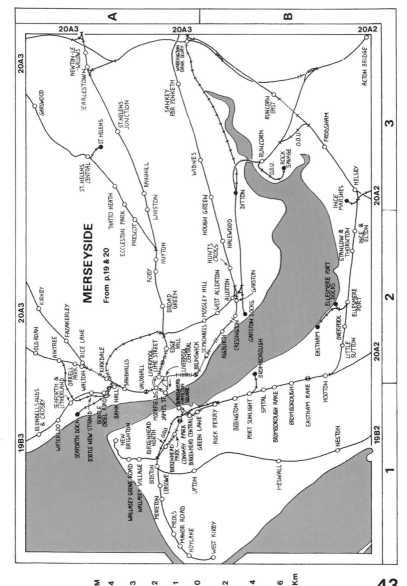

MERSEYSIDE
From p.19 & 20

43

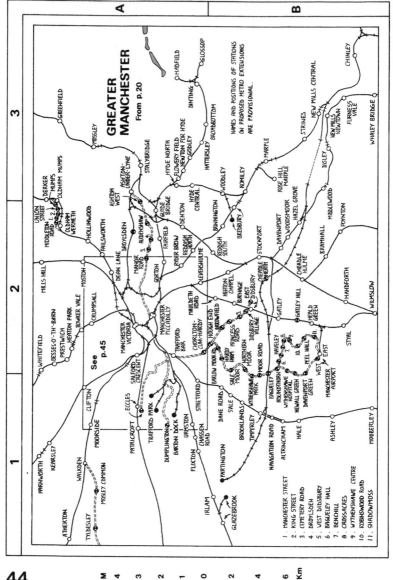

44

GREATER
MANCHESTER
From p.20

NAMES AND POSITIONS OF STATIONS
ON PROPOSED METRO EXTENSIONS
ARE PROVISIONAL.

GREENFIELD

HADFIELD

GLOSSOP

MOSSLEY

CHINLEY

DERKER

DINTING

MUMPS
OLDHAM MUMPS

STALYBRIDGE

HYDE NORTH

FLOWERY FIELD
NEWTON FOR HYDE

NEW MILLS CENTRAL

FURNESS
VALE

UNION
STREET
ROAD 1, 2
OLDHAM
WERNETH

MIDDLETON

HOLLINWOOD

ASHTON
WEST

ASHTON-
UNDER-LYNE

GUIDE
BRIDGE

GODLEY

HATTERSLEY

BROADBOTTOM

STRINES

NEW MILLS
NEWTOWN

DISLEY

WHALEY BRIDGE

MILLS HILL

FAILSWORTH

DROYLSDEN

FAIRFIELD

DENTON

HYDE
CENTRAL

BREDBURY

WOODLEY

ROMILEY

MARPLE

ROSE HILL
MARPLE

MIDDLEWOOD

POYNTON

MOSTON

DEAN LANE

MANOR
ROAD 3.

RYDER BROW

REDDISH
NORTH

REDDISH
SOUTH

HAZEL GROVE

DAVENPORT

WOODSMOOR

BRAMHALL

WHITEFIELD

BESSES-O'-TH'-BARN

PRESTWICH

HEATON PARK

BOWKER
VALE

CRUMPSALL

See
p.45

GORTON

LEVENSHULME

MAULDETH
ROAD

HEATON
CHAPEL

EAST
DIDSBURY

CHEADLE
HEATH

STOCKPORT

CHEADLE
HULME

HANDFORTH

WILMSLOW

PARKWORTH

KEARSLEY

WALKDEN

MOORSIDE

CLIFTON

ECCLES

PATRICROFT

MANCHESTER
VICTORIA

SALFORD
CRESCENT

MANCHESTER
PICCADILLY

TRAFFORD
BAR

CHORLTON-
CUM-HARDY

BURNAGE

DIDSBURY
VILLAGE

HEATON
MERSEY

GATLEY

GATLEY HILL

HEALD
GREEN

STYAL

MOBBERLEY

ATHERTON

TYLDESLEY

MOSLEY COMMON

TRAFFORD PARK

DUMPLINGTON

BARTON DOCK

URMSTON

FLIXTON

CHASSEN
ROAD

STRETFORD

DANE ROAD

SALE

BROOKLANDS

TIMPERLEY

NAVIGATION ROAD

ALTRINCHAM

HALE

ASHLEY

BROWN MOOR RD.

HARDY
FARM

SALE
MOOR

WYTHENSHAWE
PARK

BAGULEY
ROUNDTHORN

WYTHENSHAWE
HOSPITAL

NEWALL GREEN

DAVENPORT
GREEN

HOUGH END

PRINCESS
ROAD

NORTHERN
MOOR

MOOR ROAD

HAVELEY

MANCHESTER
AIRPORT

WEST

EAST

PEEL HALL

IRLAM

GLAZEBROOK

PARTINGTON

1. MANCHESTER STREET
2. KING STREET
3. CEMETERY ROAD
4. DROYLSDEN
5. WEST DIDSBURY
6. BAGULEY HALL
7. BENCHILL
8. CROSSACRES
9. WYTHENSHAWE CENTRE
10. ROBINSWOOD ROAD
11. SHADOWMOSS

M
4

3

2

1

0

2

4

6
Km

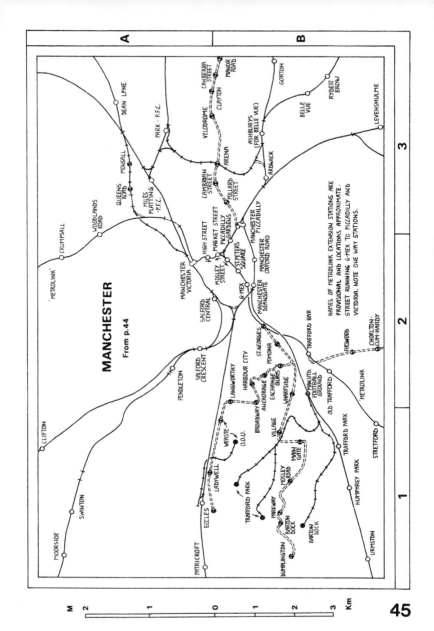

# MANCHESTER

From p.44

Names of Metrolink extension stations are provisional and locations approximate. Street running G-Mex to Piccadilly and Victoria. Note one way stations.

45

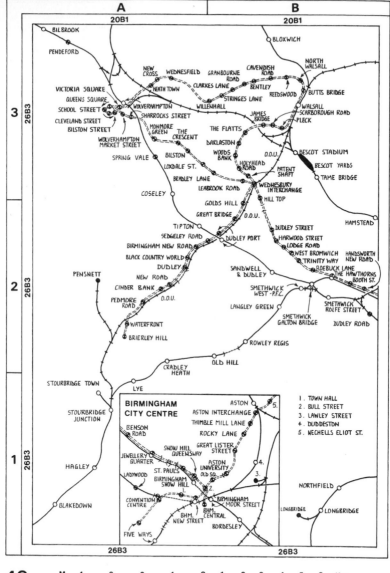

BILBROOK
PENDEFORD
BLOXWICH
NEW CROSS
WEDNESFIELD
GRANBOURNE ROAD
CAVENDISH ROAD
NORTH WALSALL
HEATH TOWN
CLARKES LANE
BENTLEY
REEDSWOOD
BUTTS BRIDGE
VICTORIA SQUARE
QUEENS SQUARE
SCHOOL STREET
STRINGES LANE
WILLENHALL
WALSALL
SCARBOROUGH ROAD
PLECK
WOLVERHAMPTON
SHARROCKS STREET
JAMES BRIDGE
CLEVELAND STREET
BILSTON STREET
MONMORE GREEN
THE CRESCENT
THE FLATTS
WOLVERHAMPTON MARKET STREET
DARLASTON
BESCOT STADIUM
BILSTON
WOODS BANK
HOLYHEAD ROAD
D.D.U.
BESCOT YARDS
SPRING VALE
LOXDALE ST.
PATENT SHAFT
TAME BRIDGE
BRADLEY LANE
LEABROOK ROAD
WEDNESBURY INTERCHANGE
COSELEY
GOLDS HILL
HILL TOP
GREAT BRIDGE
D.D.U.
HAMSTEAD
TIPTON
SEDGELEY ROAD
DUDLEY STREET
BIRMINGHAM NEW ROAD
DUDLEY PORT
HARWOOD STREET
LODGE ROAD
BLACK COUNTRY WORLD
WEST BROMWICH
TRINITY WAY
HANDSWORTH NEW ROAD
DUDLEY
SANDWELL & DUDLEY
ROEBUCK LANE
THE HAWTHORNS
BOOTH ST.
PENSNETT
NEW ROAD
SMETHWICK WEST · P.F.C.
CINDER BANK
PEDMORE ROAD
D.D.U.
LANGLEY GREEN
SMETHWICK ROLFE STREET
DUDLEY ROAD
SMETHWICK GALTON BRIDGE
WATERFRONT
BRIERLEY HILL
ROWLEY REGIS
OLD HILL
CRADLEY HEATH
STOURBRIDGE TOWN
LYE

1. TOWN HALL
2. BULL STREET
3. LAWLEY STREET
4. DUDDESTON
5. NECHELLS ELIOT ST.

**BIRMINGHAM CITY CENTRE**

ASTON
ASTON INTERCHANGE
THIMBLE MILL LANE
ROCKY LANE
BENSON ROAD
SNOW HILL QUEENSWAY
GREAT LISTER STREET
JEWELLERY QUARTER
ST. PAUL'S
ASTON UNIVERSITY
OLD SQ.
LADYWOOD
BIRMINGHAM SNOW HILL
STOURBRIDGE JUNCTION
HAGLEY
CONVENTION CENTRE
BIRMINGHAM MOOR STREET
NORTHFIELD
BLAKEDOWN
BHM. NEW STREET
BHM. CENTRAL
BORDESLEY
LONGBRIDGE
LONGBRIDGE
FIVE WAYS

A    20B1
B    20B1
26B3
26B3
26B3
26B3    26B3

46    M  4  3  2  1  0  1  2  3  4  5  6  Km

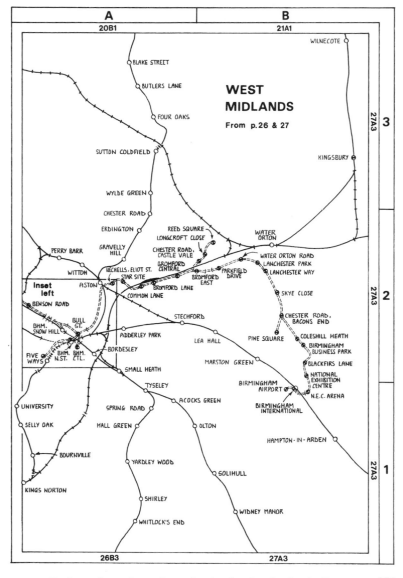

WILNECOTE

BLAKE STREET

BUTLERS LANE

**WEST MIDLANDS**

From p.26 & 27

FOUR OAKS

SUTTON COLDFIELD

KINGSBURY

27A3   3

WYLDE GREEN

CHESTER ROAD

ERDINGTON

REED SQUARE
LONGCROFT CLOSE

GRAVELLY HILL

CHESTER ROAD,
CASTLE VALE

WATER ORTON

PERRY BARR

BROMFORD
CENTRAL

WATER ORTON ROAD
LANCHESTER PARK
LANCHESTER WAY

WITTON

NECHELLS, ELIOT ST.

PARKFIELD
DRIVE

STAR SITE

ASTON

BROMFORD
EAST

**Inset
left**

BROMFORD LANE

COMMON LANE

SKYE CLOSE

27A3   2

BENSON ROAD

STECHFORD

CHESTER ROAD,
BACONS END

BHM.
SNOW HILL

BULL
ST.

ADDERLEY PARK

LEA HALL

PINE SQUARE

COLESHILL HEATH

FIVE
WAYS

BHM.
N.ST.

BHM.
CTL.

BORDESLEY

BIRMINGHAM
BUSINESS PARK

MARSTON GREEN

BLACKFIRS LANE

SMALL HEATH

TYSELEY

BIRMINGHAM
AIRPORT

NATIONAL
EXHIBITION
CENTRE

UNIVERSITY

SPRING ROAD

ACOCKS GREEN

N.E.C. ARENA

BIRMINGHAM
INTERNATIONAL

SELLY OAK

HALL GREEN

OLTON

BOURNVILLE

HAMPTON-IN-ARDEN

27A3   1

YARDLEY WOOD

SOLIHULL

KINGS NORTON

SHIRLEY

WIDNEY MANOR

WHITLOCK'S END

M   4   3   2   1   0   1   2   3   4   5   6   Km

**47**

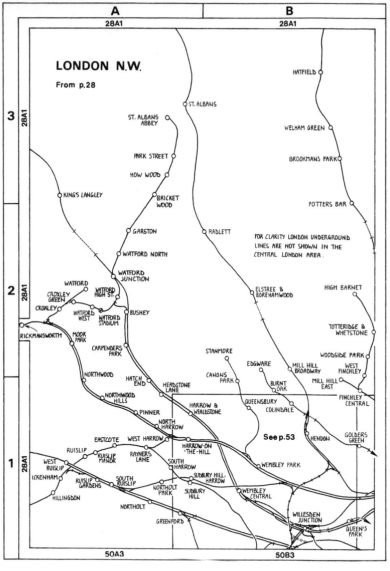

# LONDON N.W.

**From p.28**

HATFIELD

ST. ALBANS

ST. ALBANS ABBEY

WELHAM GREEN

BROOKMANS PARK

PARK STREET

HOW WOOD

KING'S LANGLEY

BRICKET WOOD

POTTERS BAR

GARSTON

RADLETT

FOR CLARITY LONDON UNDERGROUND
LINES ARE NOT SHOWN IN THE
CENTRAL LONDON AREA.

WATFORD NORTH

WATFORD JUNCTION

WATFORD

WATFORD HIGH ST.

ELSTREE & BOREHAMWOOD

HIGH BARNET

CROXLEY GREEN

CROXLEY

WATFORD WEST

BUSHEY

WATFORD STADIUM

TOTTERIDGE & WHETSTONE

RICKMANSWORTH

MOOR PARK

CARPENDERS PARK

WOODSIDE PARK

STANMORE

EDGWARE

MILL HILL BROADWAY

WEST FINCHLEY

NORTHWOOD

HATCH END

HEADSTONE LANE

CANONS PARK

BURNT OAK

MILL HILL EAST

NORTHWOOD HILLS

PINNER

HARROW & WEALDSTONE

QUEENSBURY

COLINDALE

FINCHLEY CENTRAL

EASTCOTE

WEST HARROW

NORTH HARROW

See p.53

HENDON

GOLDERS GREEN

RUISLIP

RUISLIP MANOR

RAYNERS LANE

HARROW-ON-THE-HILL

WEST RUISLIP

SOUTH HARROW

ICKENHAM

RUISLIP GARDENS

SOUTH RUISLIP

SUDBURY HILL, HARROW

WEMBLEY PARK

HILLINGDON

NORTHOLT PARK

SUDBURY HILL

WEMBLEY CENTRAL

NORTHOLT

WILLESDEN JUNCTION

GREENFORD

QUEEN'S PARK

M 3 2 1 0 1 2 3 4 Km

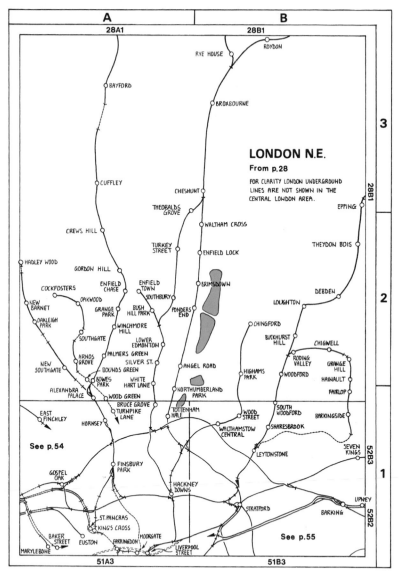

# LONDON N.E.

## From p.28

FOR CLARITY LONDON UNDERGROUND
LINES ARE NOT SHOWN IN THE
CENTRAL LONDON AREA.

See p.54

See p.55

M  3   2   1   0   1   2   3   4  Km

**49**

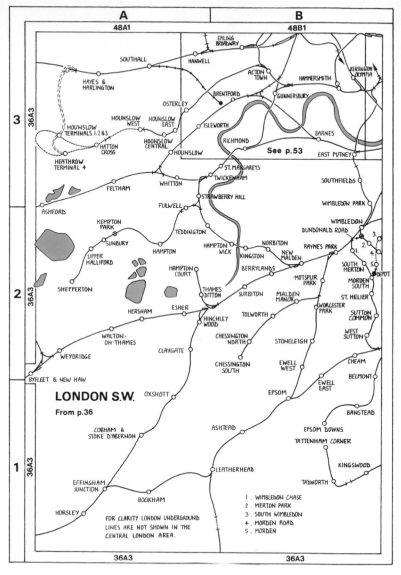

SOUTHALL HANWELL

EALING & BROADWAY

ACTON TOWN HAMMERSMITH

KENSINGTON OLYMPIA

HAYES & HARLINGTON

BRENTFORD

OSTERLEY GUNNERSBURY

HOUNSLOW WEST HOUNSLOW EAST

ISLEWORTH

BARNES

HOUNSLOW TERMINALS 1,2 & 3

HOUNSLOW CENTRAL

RICHMOND

See p.53

HATTON CROSS

HOUNSLOW

EAST PUTNEY

HEATHROW TERMINAL 4

ST. MARGARETS

SOUTHFIELDS

FELTHAM

WHITTON

TWICKENHAM

WIMBLEDON PARK

ASHFORD

FULWELL

STRAWBERRY HILL

WIMBLEDON

KEMPTON PARK

TEDDINGTON

DUNDONALD ROAD

3.

SUNBURY

HAMPTON

HAMPTON WICK

NORBITON

RAYNES PARK

2.

UPPER HALLIFORD

KINGSTON

NEW MALDEN

1.

4.

SOUTH MERTON

5.

SHEPPERTON

HAMPTON COURT

BERRYLANDS

MOTSPUR PARK

DEPOT

MORDEN SOUTH

THAMES DITTON

SURBITON

MALDEN MANOR

ST. HELIER

HERSHAM

ESHER

WORCESTER PARK

SUTTON COMMON

HINCHLEY WOOD

TOLWORTH

WALTON-ON-THAMES

WEST SUTTON

CHESSINGTON NORTH

STONELEIGH

WEYBRIDGE

CLAYGATE

CHEAM

CHESSINGTON SOUTH

EWELL WEST

BELMONT

BYFLEET & NEW HAW

OXSHOTT

EWELL EAST

EPSOM

**LONDON S.W.**

From p.36

BANSTEAD

COBHAM & STOKE D'ABERNON

ASHTEAD

EPSOM DOWNS

TATTENHAM CORNER

KINGSWOOD

EFFINGHAM JUNCTION

LEATHERHEAD

TADWORTH

HORSLEY

BOOKHAM

FOR CLARITY LONDON UNDERGROUND LINES ARE NOT SHOWN IN THE CENTRAL LONDON AREA.

1. WIMBLEDON CHASE
2. MERTON PARK
3. SOUTH WIMBLEDON
4. MORDEN ROAD
5. MORDEN

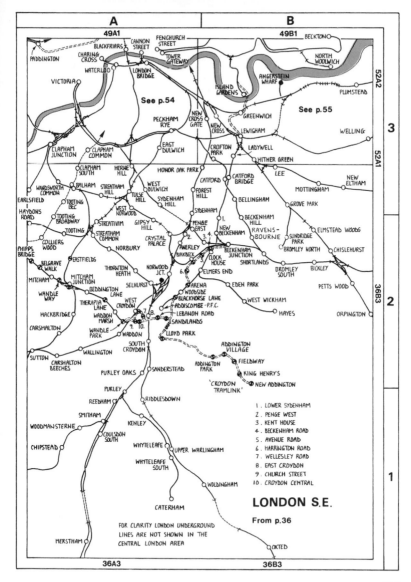

# LONDON S.E.

From p.36

1. LOWER SYDENHAM
2. PENGE WEST
3. KENT HOUSE
4. BECKENHAM ROAD
5. AVENUE ROAD
6. HARRINGTON ROAD
7. WELLESLEY ROAD
8. EAST CROYDON
9. CHURCH STREET
10. CROYDON CENTRAL

FOR CLARITY LONDON UNDERGROUND LINES ARE NOT SHOWN IN THE CENTRAL LONDON AREA

See p.54

See p.55

'CROYDON TRAMLINK'

M 3 2 1 0 1 2 3 4 Km

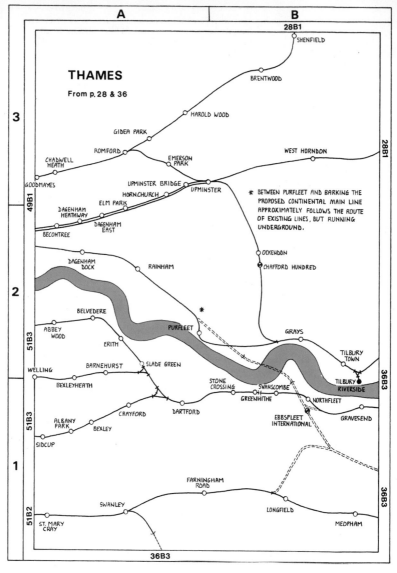

THAMES

From p. 28 & 36

* BETWEEN PURFLEET AND BARKING THE
PROPOSED CONTINENTAL MAIN LINE
APPROXIMATELY FOLLOWS THE ROUTE
OF EXISTING LINES, BUT RUNNING
UNDERGROUND.

A

B

28B1

SHENFIELD

BRENTWOOD

HAROLD WOOD

GIDEA PARK

ROMFORD

WEST HORNDON

CHADWELL HEATH

EMERSON PARK

GOODMAYES

UPMINSTER BRIDGE

HORNCHURCH

UPMINSTER

ELM PARK

DAGENHAM HEATHWAY

DAGENHAM EAST

BECONTREE

OCKENDON

CHAFFORD HUNDRED

DAGENHAM DOCK

RAINHAM

BELVEDERE

PURFLEET

GRAYS

ABBEY WOOD

TILBURY TOWN

ERITH

TILBURY RIVERSIDE

WELLING

BARNEHURST

SLADE GREEN

STONE CROSSING

SWANSCOMBE

BEXLEYHEATH

GREENHITHE

NORTHFLEET

DARTFORD

ALBANY PARK

CRAYFORD

EBBSFLEET INTERNATIONAL

GRAVESEND

BEXLEY

SIDCUP

FARNINGHAM ROAD

SWANLEY

LONGFIELD

ST. MARY CRAY

MEDPHAM

49B1

51B3

51B3

51B2

28B1

36B3

36B3

36B3

52

M 3 2 1 0 1 2 3 4 Km

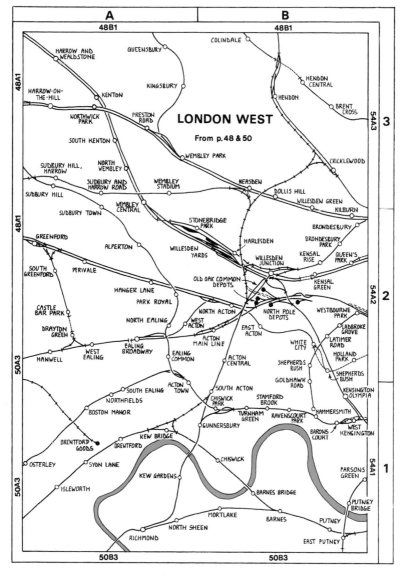

COLINDALE

HARROW AND
WEALDSTONE

QUEENSBURY

HENDON
CENTRAL

KINGSBURY

HARROW-ON-
THE-HILL

KENTON

HENDON

BRENT
CROSS

PRESTON
ROAD

NORTHWICK
PARK

**LONDON WEST**

From p.48 & 50

SOUTH KENTON

WEMBLEY PARK

CRICKLEWOOD

SUDBURY HILL,
HARROW

NORTH
WEMBLEY

SUDBURY AND
HARROW ROAD

WEMBLEY
STADIUM

NEASDEN

DOLLIS HILL

WILLESDEN GREEN

SUDBURY HILL

WEMBLEY
CENTRAL

KILBURN

SUDBURY TOWN

STONEBRIDGE
PARK

HARLESDEN

BRONDESBURY

GREENFORD

ALPERTON

WILLESDEN
YARDS

BRONDESBURY
PARK

QUEEN'S
PARK

SOUTH
GREENFORD

PERIVALE

WILLESDEN
JUNCTION

KENSAL
RISE

OLD OAK COMMON
DEPOTS

KENSAL
GREEN

HANGER LANE

CASTLE
BAR PARK

PARK ROYAL

NORTH ACTON

NORTH POLE
DEPOTS

WESTBOURNE
PARK

DRAYTON
GREEN

NORTH EALING

WEST
ACTON

EAST
ACTON

LADBROKE
GROVE

LATIMER
ROAD

HANWELL

WEST
EALING

EALING
BROADWAY

ACTON
MAIN LINE

WHITE
CITY

HOLLAND
PARK

EALING
COMMON

ACTON
CENTRAL

SHEPHERDS
BUSH

SHEPHERDS
BUSH

SOUTH EALING

ACTON
TOWN

SOUTH ACTON

GOLDHAWK
ROAD

KENSINGTON
OLYMPIA

NORTHFIELDS

CHISWICK
PARK

STAMFORD
BROOK

BOSTON MANOR

TURNHAM
GREEN

RAVENSCOURT
PARK

HAMMERSMITH

GUNNERSBURY

BARONS
COURT

WEST
KENSINGTON

BRENTFORD
GOODS

KEW BRIDGE

BRENTFORD

CHISWICK

PARSONS
GREEN

OSTERLEY

SYON LANE

KEW GARDENS

BARNES BRIDGE

PUTNEY
BRIDGE

ISLEWORTH

MORTLAKE

BARNES

PUTNEY

NORTH SHEEN

RICHMOND

EAST PUTNEY

M   2        1        0        1        2        3   Km

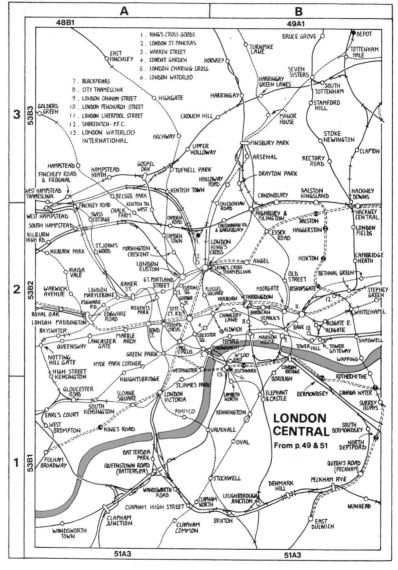

1 . KING'S CROSS GOODS
2 . LONDON ST. PANCRAS
3 . WARREN STREET
4 . COVENT GARDEN
5 . LONDON CHARING CROSS
6 . LONDON WATERLOO

7 . BLACKFRIARS
8 . CITY THAMESLINK
9 . LONDON CANNON STREET
10 . LONDON FENCHURCH STREET
11 . LONDON LIVERPOOL STREET
12 . SHOREDITCH - P.F.C.
13 . LONDON WATERLOO
      INTERNATIONAL

**LONDON CENTRAL**

From p.49 & 51

51A3          51A3

**54**    M   2     1     0     1     2     3   Km

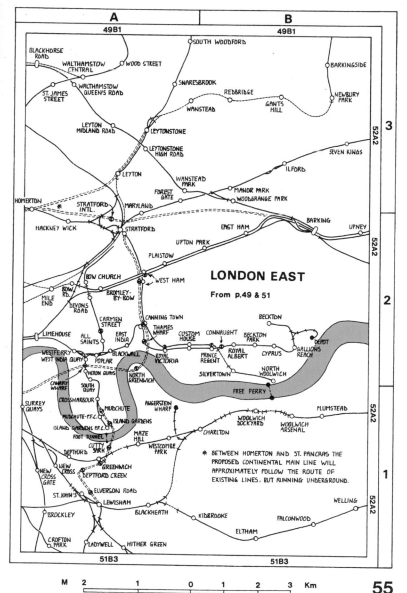

# LONDON EAST

From p.49 & 51

BLACKHORSE ROAD
WALTHAMSTOW CENTRAL
WOOD STREET
SOUTH WOODFORD
BARKINGSIDE
NEWBURY PARK
ST. JAMES STREET
WALTHAMSTOW QUEEN'S ROAD
SNARESBROOK
REDBRIDGE
GANTS HILL
WANSTEAD
LEYTON MIDLAND ROAD
LEYTONSTONE
LEYTONSTONE HIGH ROAD
SEVEN KINGS
ILFORD
LEYTON
WANSTEAD PARK
FOREST GATE
MANOR PARK
WOODGRANGE PARK
HOMERTON
STRATFORD INTL.
MARYLAND
BARKING
UPNEY
HACKNEY WICK
STRATFORD
EAST HAM
UPTON PARK
PLAISTOW
BOW CHURCH
WEST HAM
BOW RD.
BROMLEY-BY-BOW
MILE END
DEVONS ROAD
CARMEN STREET
CANNING TOWN
BECKTON
LIMEHOUSE
ALL SAINTS
EAST INDIA
THAMES WHARF
CUSTOM HOUSE
CONNAUGHT
BECKTON PARK
DEPOT
GALLIONS REACH
WESTFERRY
WEST INDIA QUAY
BLACKWALL
POPLAR
ROYAL VICTORIA
PRINCE REGENT
ROYAL ALBERT
CYPRUS
CANARY WHARF
HERON QUAYS
SOUTH QUAY
NORTH GREENWICH
SILVERTOWN
NORTH WOOLWICH
SURREY QUAYS
CROSSHARBOUR
MUDCHUTE
ANGERSTEIN WHARF
FREE FERRY
PLUMSTEAD
MUDCHUTE P.F.C.
ISLAND GARDENS P.F.C.
ISLAND GARDENS
FOOT TUNNEL
CUTTY SARK
MAZE HILL
WOOLWICH DOCKYARD
WOOLWICH ARSENAL
DEPTFORD
WESTCOMBE PARK
CHARLTON
NEW CROSS
GREENWICH
DEPTFORD CREEK
NEW CROSS GATE
ST. JOHN'S
ELVERSON ROAD
LEWISHAM
WELLING
BROCKLEY
BLACKHEATH
KIDBROOKE
FALCONWOOD
CROFTON PARK
LADYWELL
HITHER GREEN
ELTHAM

\* BETWEEN HOMERTON AND ST. PANCRAS THE PROPOSED CONTINENTAL MAIN LINE WILL APPROXIMATELY FOLLOW THE ROUTE OF EXISTING LINES, BUT RUNNING UNDERGROUND.

M 2   1   0   1   2   3 Km

# INDEX

## ENGLAND – SCOTLAND – WALES

| | |
|---|---|
| 14A1 | Laxey |
| 14B1 | Layton |
| 15A3 | Lazonby & Kirkoswald |
| 47B2 | Lea Hall |
| 46B3 | Leabrook Road |
| 28A2 | Leagrave |
| 16B3 | Lealholm |
| 27A3 | Leamington Spa |
| 43A1 | Leasowe |
| 50B1 | Leatherhead |
| 51A2 | Lebanon Road |
| 26A2 | Ledbury |
| 51B3 | Lee |
| 42A2 | Leeds |
| 21B1 | Leicester |
| 21A1 | Leicester Forest East |
| 21B1 | Leicester North |
| 54A2 | Leicester Square |
| 20A3 | Leigh (Gtr.Man.) |
| 36B3 | Leigh (Kent) |
| 29A1 | Leigh-on-Sea |
| 27B2 | Leighton Buzzard |
| 30A3 | Lelant |
| 30A3 | Lelant Saltings |
| 1A2 | Lenzie |
| 26A2 | Leominster |
| 23A3 | Leppings Lane |
| 28A2 | Letchworth |
| 9A2 | Leuchars for St.Andrews |
| 45B3 | Levenshulme |
| 16B2 | Levisham |
| 14B2 | Lewaigue |
| 36B2 | Lewes |
| 55A1 | Lewisham |
| 15B2 | Leyburn |
| 20A3 | Leyland |
| 55A3 | Leyton |
| 55A3 | Leyton Midland Road |
| 55A3 | Leytonstone |
| 55A3 | Leytonstone High Road |
| 20B1 | Lichfield City |
| 20B1 | Lichfield Trent Valley |
| 28A2 | Lidlington |
| 55A2 | Limehouse |
| 22A2 | Lincoln |
| 36B3 | Lingfield |
| 23B1 | Lingwood |
| 8B1 | Linlithgow |
| 35B2 | Liphook |
| 31A3 | Liskeard |
| 35B2 | Liss |
| 25B1 | Lisvane & Thornhill |
| 27B1 | Little Kimble |
| 43B2 | Little Sutton |
| 20B3 | Littleborough |
| 36A2 | Littlehampton |
| 36A2 | Littlehaven |
| 31B3 | Littlehempston Riverside |
| 28B3 | Littleport |
| 43A2 | Liverpool Central |
| 43A2 | Liverpool Lime Street |
| 54B2 | Liverpool Street (London) |
| 8B1 | Livingston North |
| 11B3 | Livingstone South |
| 19A1 | Llanaber |
| 25A3 | Llanbadarn |
| 19A1 | Llanbedr |
| 19A2 | Llanberis |
| 25B3 | Llanbister Road |
| 25B1 | Llanbradach |
| 32A3 | Llandaff |

| | |
|---|---|
| 19A1 | Llandanwg |
| 18A3 | Llandecwyn |
| 25A1 | Llandeilo |
| 25A2 | Llandovery |
| 25B2 | Llandrindod |
| 19A2 | Llandudno |
| 19A2 | Llandudno Junction |
| 19A2 | Llandudno Victoria |
| 25A1 | Llandybie |
| 24B2 | Llandyfriog |
| 24B1 | Llanelli |
| 19B1 | Llanfair Caereinion |
| 19A2 | Llanfairfechan |
| 18B2 | Llanfairpwll * |
| 25A2 | Llangadog |
| 25B2 | Llangammarch |
| 25A1 | Llangennech |
| 19B1 | Llangollen |
| 19A1 | Llangower |
| 25B3 | Llangynllo |
| 25A3 | Llanilar |
| 32A3 | Llanishen |
| 25A3 | Llanrhystyd Road |
| 19A2 | Llanrwst |
| 19A2 | Llanrwst North |
| 25A1 | Llansamlet |
| 19A1 | Llanuwchllyn |
| 25A2 | Llanwrda |
| 25A2 | Llanwrtyd |
| 51A2 | Lloyd Park |
| 24B2 | Llwyfan Cerrig |
| 19A1 | Llwyngwril |
| 25B1 | Llwynypia |
| 7B2 | Loch Awe |
| 7B3 | Loch Eil Outward Bound |
| 7A3 | Lochailort |
| 7A3 | Locheilside |
| 8B1 | Lochgelly |
| 4B2 | Lochluichart |
| 10B3 | Lochwinnoch |
| 11B1 | Lockerbie |
| 42B1 | Lockwood |
| 20B3 | Lockwood |
| 46B2 | Lodge Road |
| 54B2 | London Blackfriars |
| 54B2 | London Bridge |
| 54B2 | London Canon Street |
| 54A2 | London Charing Cross |
| 54A2 | London Euston |
| 54B2 | London Fenchurch Street |
| 54B2 | London Fields |
| 54A2 | London King's Cross |
| 54B2 | London Liverpool Street |
| 54A2 | London Marylebone |
| 54A2 | London Paddington |
| 36A1 | London Road (Brighton) |
| 36A3 | London Road (Guildford) |
| 54A2 | London St.Pancras |
| 54A1 | London Victoria |
| 54B2 | London Waterloo |
| 54B2 | London Waterloo International |
| 27B3 | Long Buckby |
| 21A1 | Long Eaton |
| 15B1 | Long Preston |
| 16B3 | Longbeck |
| 13A3 | Longbenton |
| 46B1 | Longbridge |
| 47B2 | Longcroft Close |
| 36A3 | Longcross |
| 52B1 | Longfield |
| 9A1 | Longniddry |

* Abbreviation of:
Llanfairpwllgwyngyllgogerychwyrndrobwllllantysiliogogogoch
Also known as Llanfair P.G.

| | |
|---|---|
| 16A3 | North Road |
| 53A1 | North Sheen |
| 13B3 | North Shields |
| 46B3 | North Walsall |
| 23B1 | North Walsham |
| 28B1 | North Weald |
| 53A3 | North Wembley |
| 55B2 | North Woolwich |
| 16A2 | Northallerton |
| 27B2 | Northampton |
| 44B2 | Northern Moor |
| 46B1 | Northfield |
| 53A1 | Northfields |
| 52B1 | Northfleet |
| 37A2 | Northiam |
| 48A1 | Northolt |
| 48A1 | Northolt Park |
| 49A1 | Northumberland Park |
| 20A2 | Northwich |
| 53A3 | Northwick Park |
| 21A2 | Northwood (Derbys.) |
| 48A1 | Northwood (Gtr.London) |
| 26B3 | Northwood Halt (Worcs.) |
| 48A1 | Northwood Hills |
| 20B1 | Norton Bridge |
| 23B1 | Norwich |
| 51A2 | Norwood Junction |
| 54A2 | Notting Hill Gate |
| 21B1 | Nottingham |
| 27A3 | Nuneaton |
| 54B1 | Nunhead |
| 23A3 | Nunnery |
| 29A2 | Nunnery Halt |
| 16A3 | Nunthorpe |
| 35B2 | Nutbourne |
| 36A3 | Nutfield |
| 20A1 | Oakengates |
| 21B1 | Oakham |
| 49A2 | Oakleigh Park |
| 49A2 | Oakwood |
| 15B1 | Oakworth |
| 7A2 | Oban |
| 52B2 | Ockendon |
| 36A2 | Ockley |
| 33A1 | Okehampton |
| 46B2 | Old Hill |
| 43A2 | Old Roan |
| 46B1 | Old Square |
| 54B2 | Old Street |
| 45B2 | Old Trafford |
| 34B3 | Oldfield Park |
| 44A3 | Oldham Mumps |
| 44A2 | Oldham Werneth |
| 34A3 | Oldland Common |
| 47A1 | Olton |
| 14A1 | Onchan Head |
| 28B1 | Ongar |
| 37A2 | Ore |
| 20A3 | Ormskirk |
| 51B2 | Orpington |
| 20A3 | Orrell |
| 43A2 | Orrell Park |
| 28A3 | Orton Mere |
| 53A1 | Osterley |
| 36B3 | Otford |
| 29B3 | Oulton Broad North |
| 29B3 | Oulton Broad South |
| 42B2 | Outwood |
| 54B1 | Oval |
| 43B2 | Overpool |
| 35A3 | Overton |
| 15A2 | Oxenholme, Lake District |
| 15B1 | Oxenhope |
| 27A1 | Oxford |
| 54A2 | Oxford Road |
| 50A1 | Oxshott |
| 51B1 | Oxted |
| 54A2 | Paddington (London) |
| 36B3 | Paddock Wood |
| 20A3 | Padgate |
| 27B2 | Page's Park |
| 31B3 | Paignton |
| 31B3 | Paignton Queen's Park |
| 1B1 | Paisley Canal |
| 1B1 | Paisley Gilmour Street |
| 1B1 | Paisley St.James |
| 13A1 | Pallion |
| 49A2 | Palmers Green |
| 13B3 | Palmersville |
| 35B3 | Pangbourne |
| 16A1 | Pannal |
| 25B1 | Pant |
| 25A1 | Pantyffynnon |
| 30B3 | Par |
| 20A3 | Parbold |
| 45A3 | Park |
| 23A2 | Park Grange |
| 21A1 | Park Rise |
| 53A2 | Park Royal |
| 23A3 | Park Square |
| 48A3 | Park Street |
| 47B2 | Parkfield Drive |
| 34B1 | Parkstone |
| 45B1 | Parkway |
| 32A1 | Parson Street |
| 53B1 | Parsons Green |
| 2A3 | Partick |
| 14B3 | Parton |
| 32A2 | Patchway |
| 46B3 | Patent Shaft |
| 45A1 | Patricroft |
| 1B1 | Patterton |
| 21A1 | Peartree |
| 54B1 | Peckham Rye |
| 46A2 | Pedmore Road |
| 44B2 | Peel Hall |
| 13A2 | Pegswood |
| 13B3 | Pelaw |
| 20A3 | Pemberton |
| 24B1 | Pembrey & Burry Port |
| 24A1 | Pembroke |
| 24A1 | Pembroke Dock |
| 25B3 | Pen-y-Bont |
| 18A3 | Pen-y-Mount |
| 24B1 | Penally |
| 32A1 | Penarth |
| 33B3 | Pencoed |
| 46A3 | Pendeford |
| 45A2 | Pendleton |
| 25B1 | Pengam |
| 51A2 | Penge East |
| 51A2 | Penge West |
| 25A3 | Penhelig |
| 21A3 | Penistone |
| 20B1 | Penkridge |
| 19A2 | Penmaenmawr |
| 30B2 | Penmere |
| 25B1 | Penrhiwceiber |
| 18A3 | Penrhyn (Gwynedd) |
| 18A3 | Penrhyndeudraeth |
| 15A3 | Penrith |
| 30B3 | Penryn (Cornwall) |
| 19A1 | Pensarn |
| 36B3 | Penshurst |
| 19A1 | Pentepiod |
| 25B1 | Pentre Bach |
| 18B1 | Penychain |
| 19B2 | Penyffordd |
| 30A2 | Penzance |
| 13B3 | Percy Main |
| 13B3 | Percy Main North |
| 53A2 | Perivale |

| | |
|---|---|
| 16B3 | Redcar Central |
| 16B3 | Redcar East |
| 44A2 | Reddish North |
| 44B2 | Reddish South |
| 26B3 | Redditch |
| 36A3 | Redhill |
| 32A2 | Redland |
| 15B2 | Redmire |
| 30A3 | Redruth |
| 47B2 | Reed Square |
| 23B1 | Reedham (Norfolk) |
| 51A1 | Reedham (Gtr.London) |
| 46B3 | Reedswood |
| 13A3 | Regent Centre |
| 54A2 | Regents Park |
| 36A3 | Reigate |
| 7B1 | Renton |
| 21B2 | Retford |
| 25A3 | Rheidol Falls |
| 32A3 | Rhiwbina |
| 25A3 | Rhiwfron |
| 18B2 | Rhosneigr |
| 19A2 | Rhyd-Ddu |
| 25A3 | Rhydyronen |
| 19B2 | Rhyl |
| 25B1 | Rhymney |
| 15A2 | Ribblehead |
| 43A2 | Rice Lane |
| 53A1 | Richmond |
| 28A1 | Rickmansworth |
| 51A1 | Riddlesdown |
| 28A2 | Ridgmont |
| 12B1 | Riding Mill |
| 15A1 | Rishton |
| 27B2 | Roade |
| 36B2 | Robertsbridge |
| 44B2 | Robinswood Road |
| 43A2 | Roby |
| 20B3 | Rochdale |
| 20B3 | Rochdale Town Centre |
| 30B3 | Roche |
| 37B1 | Rochester |
| 29A1 | Rochford |
| 43B1 | Rock Ferry |
| 46B1 | Rocky Lane |
| 19A2 | Rocky Valley Halt |
| 49B2 | Roding Valley |
| 46B2 | Roebuck Lane |
| 5A3 | Rogart |
| 13A1 | Roker |
| 21B2 | Rolleston |
| 37A2 | Rolvenden |
| 19A2 | Roman Bridge |
| 52A3 | Romford |
| 44B3 | Romiley |
| 37A2 | Romney Sands |
| 35A2 | Romsey |
| 14B2 | Roose |
| 35B2 | Ropley |
| 15B1 | Rose Grove |
| 44B3 | Rose Hill Marple |
| 8B1 | Rosyth |
| 23B3 | Rotherham Central |
| 54B2 | Rotherhithe |
| 21B1 | Rothley |
| 23B2 | Roughton Road |
| 44B2 | Roundthorne |
| 35B2 | Rowlands Castle |
| 46B2 | Rowley Regis |
| 7B3 | Roy Bridge |
| 55B2 | Royal Albert |
| 54A2 | Royal Oak |
| 55A2 | Royal Victoria |
| 49B3 | Roydon |
| 28A2 | Royston |
| 19B2 | Ruabon |

| | |
|---|---|
| 21B1 | Ruddington |
| 20A3 | Rufford |
| 27A3 | Rugby |
| 20B1 | Rugeley |
| 48A1 | Ruislip |
| 48A1 | Ruislip Gardens |
| 48A1 | Ruislip Manor |
| 43B3 | Runcorn |
| 43B3 | Runcorn East |
| 21A1 | Rushcliffe Halt |
| 22A2 | Ruskington |
| 54A2 | Russell Square |
| 16B3 | Ruswarp |
| 2B2 | Rutherglen |
| 35B1 | Ryde Esplanade |
| 35B1 | Ryde Pierhead |
| 35B1 | Ryde St.John's |
| 45B3 | Ryder Brow |
| 37A2 | Rye |
| 49B3 | Rye House |
| 10B3 | Salcoats |
| 44B1 | Sale |
| 44B2 | Sale Moor |
| 45B2 | Salford Central |
| 45A2 | Salford Crescent |
| 36A3 | Salfords |
| 23B1 | Salhouse |
| 35A2 | Salisbury |
| 42A1 | Saltaire |
| 31A2 | Saltash |
| 16B3 | Saltburn |
| 42B1 | Salterhebble |
| 16B1 | Saltmarshe |
| 15A1 | Salwick |
| 42B3 | Sandal & Agbrigg |
| 20A2 | Sandbach |
| 51A2 | Sanderstead |
| 43A1 | Sandhills |
| 35B3 | Sandhurst |
| 51A2 | Sandilands |
| 37A2 | Sandling |
| 35B1 | Sandown |
| 31A3 | Sandplace |
| 46B2 | Sandwell & Dudley |
| 37B3 | Sandwich |
| 28A2 | Sandy |
| 43A3 | Sankey for Penketh |
| 11A2 | Sanquhar |
| 14A1 | Santon |
| 33A3 | Sarn |
| 24B1 | Saundersfoot |
| 27B1 | Saunderton |
| 28B1 | Sawbridgeworth |
| 21B2 | Saxilby |
| 29B3 | Saxmundham |
| 17A2 | Scarborough |
| 46B3 | Scarborough Road |
| 46A3 | School Street |
| 3A2 | Scotscalder |
| 1A1 | Scotstounhill |
| 21B3 | Scunthorpe |
| 32A2 | Sea Mills |
| 13B2 | Seaburn |
| 36B1 | Seaford |
| 43A1 | Seaforth & Litherland |
| 13A1 | Seaham |
| 17A2 | Seamer |
| 14B2 | Seascale |
| 33B1 | Seaton |
| 16A3 | Seaton Carew |
| 46B2 | Sedgeley Road |
| 28A1 | Seer Green |
| 16B1 | Selby |
| 51A2 | Selhurst |
| 14B2 | Sellafield |
| 37A3 | Selling |